E X E R C I S E S

easy
Writer

fourth edition

easy Writer

fourth edition

Lex Runciman
LINFIELD COLLEGE

Carolyn Lengel

EXERCISES

BEDFORD/ST. MARTIN'S
Boston ◆ New York

Manufactured in the United States of America.

4 3 2 1 0 9
f e d c b a

For information, write: Bedford/St. Martin's, 75 Arlington Street, Boston, MA 02116
(617-399-4000)

ISBN-10: 0-312-58387-7
ISBN-13: 978-0-312-58387-3

Preface

Exercises for *EasyWriter* is a resource for teachers and students. Its exercises consist of sentences and paragraphs in need of revision; most are designed so that students can edit directly on the pages of this book.

The exercise sets are numbered to correspond to chapters in *EasyWriter*. Students can quickly locate help by following the cross-references in each exercise's instructions.

To help students check their own progress as they work, answers to the even-numbered exercise items appear in the back of this book. Exercises with many possible answers — those asking students to imitate a sentence or revise a paragraph, for example — are not answered here. Answers to the odd-numbered exercises are given in the instructor's answer key only.

If you have adopted *EasyWriter* as a text, you are welcome to photocopy any of these exercises to use for homework assignments, classroom activities, or quizzes. The book is also available for student purchase. Also available on our Web site are additional exercises for practice: **bedfordstmartins.com/easywriter**.

Contents

SENTENCE STYLE

PUNCTUATION/MECHANICS

LANGUAGE

MULTILINGUAL WRITERS

ANSWERS TO THE EVEN-NUMBERED EXERCISES

• • • • •

3.1 Using the Toulmin system

Use the seven-part Toulmin system to begin to develop an argument in response to one of the following questions. Here is the Toulmin system:

1. Make your claim.

2. Restate or qualify your claim.

3. Present good reasons to support your claim.

4. Explain the underlying assumptions that connect your claim and your reasons. If an underlying assumption is controversial, provide backing for it.

5. Provide additional grounds to support your claim.

6. Acknowledge and respond to possible counterarguments.

7. Draw a conclusion, stated as strongly as possible.

(See *EasyWriter*, 3d.)

1. Should the Pledge of Allegiance include the phrase "under God," or should that phrase be omitted?

2. Should schools be responsible for children's moral education, or should a child's moral development be solely the concern of the parents?

3.2 Recognizing arguable statements

Indicate which of the following sentences are arguable statements of opinion and which are factual by filling in the blank after each sentence with *arguable* or *factual*. (See *EasyWriter*, Chapter 3.) Example:

> **Many children in the United States and around the world do not have access to computer**
>
> **technology.** factual

1. That some children have access to this technology while others do not is unacceptable.

    _____

2. This imbalance in access is often called the "digital divide." _____

3. The digital divide is the greatest cause of inequality among children in the world today.

    _____

4. Some people believe that they can help bridge this gap by providing resources and training to

    technologically disadvantaged communities. _____

5. The nonprofit organization One Laptop per Child (OLPC) claims its purpose is to educate

    children in developing countries by providing them with appropriate technology and support.

    _____

6. This organization's brilliant idea is to give poor children simple, inexpensive computers.

    _____

7. OLPC originally stated that its goal was to create a $100 laptop, but now the aim is a $75

    laptop. _____

8. Some critics declare that the money spent on these laptops would be more effectively spent

    on books. _____

9. In the twenty-first century, technological literacy is a key part of any child's education.

    _____

10. Without access to the digital world, children will grow up unprepared for modern life.

    _____

7.3 Editing verb forms

Where necessary, edit the following sentences to eliminate any inappropriate verb forms. If the verb forms in a sentence are correct as written, write *C*. (See *EasyWriter*, 7a.) Example:

>   *began*
> She ~~begin~~ the examination on time.
>   ^

1. The backstroke racers kicked hard and swum efficiently across the pool.

2. Her grandmother had gave her a beautiful pearl necklace to wear in her wedding.

3. The band had sang its last song before the fight begun.

4. Please don't make us any dinner; we have already ate.

5. They had felt that tired only once before.

6. We tried the famous Junior's Cheesecake the last time we visited Brooklyn.

7. We brung baked beans to the potluck dinner.

8. The accountants must have knowed what the CEO was up to when he looted the company.

9. My brother growed six inches in one year!

10. Over the years, Martin has become a close friend.

7.4 Distinguishing between *lie* and *lay*, *sit* and *set*, *rise* and *raise*

Choose the appropriate verb form in each of the following sentences. (See *Easy Writer*, 7b.)
Example:

> **The boys laid/<u>lay</u> on the couch, hoping for something good on TV.**

1. I sat/set back, closed my eyes, and began to meditate.

2. Exhausted from the basketball tournament the day before, the boys spent Sunday laying/lying around and playing video games.

3. The guests raised/rose their glasses to toast the dinner party host.

4. The choir rose/raised up and belted out a hymn.

5. Sitting/Setting in the sun too long can lead to skin cancer.

6. The students sat/set their backpacks down beside their desks and stared grimly at the new teacher.

7. He used whatever was lying/laying around the house.

8. Please set/sit the grocery bags on the counter.

9. I lay/laid my books down just as the telephone rang.

10. Sometimes she just lies/lays and stares at the ceiling.

7.5 Deciding on verb tenses

Complete each of the following sentences by filling in the blank with an appropriate form of the verb given in parentheses. Because more than one form will sometimes be possible, choose one form and then be prepared to explain the reasons for your choice. (See *EasyWriter*, 7c.) Example:

> **We** _celebrated/celebrate/will celebrate/will be celebrating_ **(celebrate) Halloween on the night of**
>
> **October 31.**
>
> **The past tense *celebrated* is appropriate if the sentence refers to Halloween at a specific time in the past; the present tense *celebrate* is appropriate if the sentence states a general truth about Halloween; the simple future tense *will celebrate* is appropriate if the sentence is about a future action; the future progressive tense *will be celebrating* is appropriate if the sentence is about a future and continuing action. Any of these answers is acceptable.**

1. The tradition of Halloween _____ (come) from ancient Celtic culture.

2. The ancient Celts of Ireland and Scotland _____ (celebrate) a festival called Samhain on November 1 to mark the end of the harvest season.

3. Some students might _____ (learn) about the ancient Halloween traditions in school.

4. For example, scholars _____ (know) that Samhain was a time when the ancient pagans _____ (take) stock of their supplies before winter.

5. The people believed that ghosts, demons, and other supernatural beings _____ (come) back to life and _____ (walk) the earth.

6. They _____ (light) bonfires, _____ (make) sacrifices, and _____ (wear) masks and costumes to appease the living dead.

7. Children and adults _____ (follow) old traditions when they wear costumes.

8. The Halloween tradition of trick-or-treating _____ (resemble) the medieval practice of "mumming" often performed on the eve of All Saints' Day.

9. When next October 31 _____ (arrive), communities across the United States _____ (distribute) candy to costumed revelers.

10. Today's Halloween celebrations _____ (aim) to entertain the living rather than to appease the dead.

7.6 Sequencing tenses

Change the italicized word or phrase in each of the following sentences to create the appropriate sequence of tenses. If a sentence reads acceptably, write C. (See *EasyWriter*, 7d.) Example:

> have sent
> **He needs *to* ~~send~~ in his application before today.**
>   ^

1. The crew *had dug* the trench before they installed the cable.

2. Until I saw the sequel, I *have expected* a tragic ending.

3. Is that the play you *have told* me about in practice last week?

4. After Darius said that he wanted to postpone college, I *am trying* to talk him out of it.

5. Emily will start a blog when she *will travel* abroad next fall.

6. The senator *hoped* to be ahead in the polls by now.

7. You *will have finished* your paper by the time the semester ends.

8. When he was twenty-one, he *wanted to become* a millionaire by the age of thirty.

9. The news had just begun when our power *goes* out.

10. *Cutting off* all contact with family, he had no one to ask for help.

7.7 Converting the voice of a sentence

Convert each sentence from active to passive voice or from passive to active voice, and note the differences in emphasis these changes make. (See *EasyWriter*, 7e.) Example:

> **Machiavelli advises the prince to gain the friendship of the people.**
>
> *The prince is advised by Machiavelli to gain the friendship of the people.*

1. Usually, the highest salary in professional baseball is received by a New York Yankee.

2. The black boxes were recovered by airline officials.

3. Have any spiders been seen in the basement lately?

4. The last doughnut in the box was eaten by Jerry just a few minutes ago.

5. A decrease in the intensity of the patients' symptoms was observed by the researchers.

6. For months, the baby kangaroo is protected, fed, and taught how to survive by its mother.

7. An American teenager narrates DBC Pierre's prizewinning novel about a Columbine-like school shooting, *Vernon God Little*.

8. The lawns and rooftops were covered with the first snow of winter.

9. Marianne avoided such things as elevators, subways, and closets.

10. Suddenly, rainfall pounded on the roof over our heads.

7.8 Using the subjunctive mood

Revise any of the following sentences that do not use the appropriate subjunctive verb forms required in formal or academic writing. If the verb forms in a sentence are appropriate as printed, write C. (See *EasyWriter*, 7f.) Example:

> He moved carefully, as if he ~~was~~ *were* caring for an infant.

1. Even if I was rich, I wouldn't buy those overpriced shoes.

2. The coach demands that the team is on time.

3. The lawyer made it seem as if I was a threat to society.

4. Patrick would have run the race in Central Park on New Year's Eve if he would have heard about it in advance.

5. I wish I was with you right now.

6. It is necessary that the manager knows how to do any job in the store.

7. Her stepsisters treated Cinderella as though she was a servant.

8. The invisible announcer requested that audience members should not take photographs.

9. The only requirement is that the tense of both clauses makes sense.

10. If I would have remembered my keys, I would not have been locked out.

8.1 Selecting verbs that agree with their subjects

Underline the appropriate verb form in each of the following sentences. (See *EasyWriter*, Chapter 8.) Example:

Experts on every subject is/are easy to find on the Internet.

1. The desire to find information and answers sends/send many people on Internet searches.

2. There is/are many people eager to offer advice online.

3. What credentials does/do these so-called experts have?

4. Problems with using the Internet includes/include the difficulty of determining which sources are reliable.

5. Everyone with access to a computer and a modem has/have the ability to send information over the Internet.

6. Some people put up Web pages that offers/offer impressive but inaccurate data.

7. If a delusional science fiction buff and a respected professor of cosmology writes/write about a new comet, the latter will probably provide better research.

8. To some people, everything on the Internet looks/look equally convincing.

9. A slick design and an eye-catching graphic does/do not mean that the information provided on a Web page is accurate.

10. Learning how to navigate the Web and conduct searches does/do not take the place of developing critical thinking skills.

8.2 Making subjects and verbs agree

Revise the following sentences as necessary to establish subject-verb agreement. If a sentence does not require any change, write C. (See *EasyWriter*, Chapter 8.) Example:

> has
> A new museum displaying O. Winston Link's photographs ~~have~~ opened in Roanoke, Virginia.
>   ^

1. Anyone interested in steam locomotives have probably already heard of the photographer O. Winston Link.

2. Imagine that it are the 1950s, and Link is creating his famous photographs.

3. The steam locomotives—the "iron horses" of the nineteenth century—has begun to give way to diesel engines.

4. Only the Norfolk & Western rail line's Appalachian route still use steam engines.

5. Link, a specialist in public relations, is also a commercial photographer and train lover.

6. He and his assistant Thomas Garver sets up nighttime shots of steam locomotives.

7. Days of setup is required for a single flash photo of a train passing by.

8. Many of the photos show scenes that would have been totally in the dark without Link's flashbulbs.

9. Up to sixteen flashbulbs and specialized reflectors illuminates every important detail.

10. Link's fine photographic eye and his ability to imagine how the flash will look allows him to compose each photo in advance in the dark.

11. His book *Steam, Steel, and Stars* include most of his stunning nighttime train photographs.

12. Famous Link photos such as one of a steam engine passing a drive-in movie appear in the book.

13. Today, the photographs of O. Winston Link has a cult following.

14. More than two thousand negatives from the steam locomotive era belongs to the O. Winston Link Museum in Roanoke.

15. Almost everyone who has seen a Link photograph remembers it.

9.1 Identifying adjectives and adverbs

Identify the adjectives and adverbs in each of the following sentences, underlining the adjectives once and the adverbs twice. Remember that articles and some pronouns can function as adjectives. (See *EasyWriter*, 9a.) Example:

> <u>Uncomfortable</u> in <u>his</u> <u>increasingly</u> <u>tight</u> jeans, he rejected <u>a</u> <u>second</u> dessert.

1. Politicians must seriously consider how well their lives will withstand intense public scrutiny.

2. Her small dogs bark noisily whenever the mail carrier approaches the front door.

3. The shoes in that store are lovely, uncomfortably narrow, and much too expensive.

4. The dilapidated tour bus cruised steadily along the winding road up the steep mountain.

5. I do not want any more of your sorry excuses.

6. The youngest dancer in the troupe performed a brilliant solo.

7. The most instructive of the books is, unfortunately, the longest.

8. The guests looked eagerly toward the kitchen as delicious smells wafted through the house.

9. Late in the day, the temperature dropped precipitously.

10. The history professor talked excitedly about the fascinating rulers of the Roman Empire.

9.2 Adding adjectives and adverbs

Expand each of the following sentences by adding appropriate adjectives and adverbs. Delete *the* if need be. (See *EasyWriter*, 9a.) Example:

Then   three   thoroughly   nervous
The veterinarians examined the patient.

1. Our assignment is due Wednesday.

2. Most of us enjoy movies.

3. Her superiors praised her work for the Environmental Protection Agency.

4. The judge addresses the jury.

5. The graduate seeks employment.

6. A visitor can learn the language.

7. I have neglected my friend.

8. The media are ignoring his candidacy.

9. Nobody saw the bear, but the ranger said it was dangerous.

10. Why did the man run back to the house?

9.3 Using adjectives and adverbs appropriately

Revise each of the following sentences to correct adverb and adjective use. Then, for each adjective and adverb you've revised, point out the word that it modifies. (See *EasyWriter*, 9a.) Example:

commonly
Almost every language ~~common~~ uses nonverbal cues that people can interpret.

1. Most people understand easy that raised eyebrows indicate surprise.

2. When a man defiant crosses his arms across his chest, you probably do not need to ask what the gesture means.

3. You are sure familiar with the idea that bodily motions are a kind of language, but is the same thing true of nonverbal sounds?

4. If you feel sadly, your friends may express sympathy by saying, "Awww."

5. When food tastes well, diners express their satisfaction by murmuring, "Mmmm!"

6. If you feel relievedly that a long day is finally over, you may say, "Whew!"

7. These nonverbal signals are called "paralanguage," and they are quick becoming an important field of linguistic study.

8. Paralanguage "words" may look oddly on paper.

9. Written words can only partial indicate what paralanguage sounds like.

10. Lucky for linguists today, digital recorders are readily available.

9.4 Using comparative and superlative modifiers appropriately

Revise each of the following sentences to use modifiers correctly, clearly, and effectively. A variety of acceptable answers is possible for each sentence. (See *EasyWriter*, 9b.) Example:

> **When Macbeth and Lady Macbeth plot to kill the king, she shows herself to be the**
> *more*
> ~~most~~ **ambitious of the two.**
> ^

1. The Van Gogh painting was the most priceless.

2. Most of the elderly are women because women tend to live longer.

3. My graduation day will be the most happiest day of my life.

4. Minneapolis is the largest of the Twin Cities.

5. Many couples preparing to marry now arrange for a longer engagement.

6. St. Francis made Assisi one of the famousest towns in Italy.

7. Our team sampled Jujubes, Goldberg's Peanut Chews, and Milk Duds to see which candy was easier on our teeth.

8. That trip to the dentist for a root canal was the unpleasantest experience of my life.

9. You could have found a more nicer way to thank your grandmother for the gift.

10. She has the most unique laugh.

10.1 **Revising sentences with misplaced modifiers**

Revise each of the following sentences by moving any misplaced modifiers so that they clearly modify the words they are intended to. You may have to change grammatical structures for some sentences. (See *EasyWriter*, 10a.) Example:

> full of identical tract houses
>
> **Elderly people and students live in the neighborhood̂ surrounding the university/.**
>
> ~~which is full of identical tract houses.~~

1. Doctors recommend a new test for cancer, which is painless.

2. The tenor captivated the entire audience singing with verve.

3. I went through the process of taxiing and taking off in my mind.

4. The city approximately spent twelve million dollars on the new stadium.

5. Am I the only person who cares about modifiers in sentences that are misplaced?

6. On the day in question, the patient was not normally able to breathe.

7. Refusing to die at the end of the play, the audience stared in amazement at the actor playing Hamlet.

8. The clothes were full of holes that I was giving away.

9. Revolving out of control, the maintenance worker shut down the turbine.

10. A wailing baby was quickly kissed by the candidate with a soggy diaper.

10.2 Revising squinting modifiers, disruptive modifiers, and split infinitives

Revise each of the following sentences by moving disruptive modifiers and split infinitives as well as by repositioning any squinting modifier so that it unambiguously modifies either the word(s) before it or the word(s) after it. You may have to add words to a sentence to revise it adequately. (See *EasyWriter*, 10b.) Example:

> **The course we hoped would engross us completely bored us.**
>
> The course we hoped would completely engross us bored us.
> **OR**
> The course we hoped would engross us bored us completely.

1. Airline security personnel asked Ishmael, while he was hurrying to make his connecting flight, to remove his shoes and socks and to open his carry-on bag.

2. He remembered vividly enjoying the sound of Mrs. McIntosh's singing.

3. Sasha finally, after calling several companies, found a cheaper cell phone plan.

4. The mayor promised after her reelection she would not raise taxes.

5. The exhibit, because of extensive publicity, attracted large audiences.

6. The hardware store where we bought lightbulbs recently went out of business.

7. The scientist plans to once and for all prove that the medication is effective.

8. Doctors can now restore limbs that have been severed partially to a functioning condition.

9. A new housing development has gone up with six enormous homes on the hill across the road from Mr. Jacoby's farm.

10. The speaker said when he finished he would answer questions.

11. People who swim frequently will improve their physical condition.

12. The temperature dropped causing after a day of rain black ice to form on the roads.

13. The state commission promised at its final meeting to make its recommendations public.

14. Stella did not want to argue, after a long day at work and an evening class, about who was going to do the dishes.

15. Seeing how many people were in need, Luis offered to despite his busy teaching schedule volunteer once a month with Habitat for Humanity.

10.3 Revising dangling modifiers

Revise each of the following sentences to correct the dangling modifiers. (See *EasyWriter*, 10c.) Example:

> **By sharing it on the Internet, a video can become very popular very quickly.**
>
> *Revision*: A video can become very popular very quickly when people share it on the Internet.

1. Using email and sites like MySpace and Facebook, favorite clips are easily passed on to friends.

2. Spread to a large audience over a short period of time, people make comparisons to a virus.

3. Shooting with camera phones, many viral videos are created in minutes.

4. Usually short and often funny, entertainment is generally the reason for their existence.

5. Shot by both amateurs and professionals, the quality can vary a lot.

6. Using simple equipment and editing techniques, even home movies can become viral videos.

7. Ignoring copyright laws, material created by others may be distributed as well.

8. To share funny moments from TV shows, clips are posted on video-sharing sites.

9. Looking at sites such as YouTube, millions of these short films and excerpts can be found.

10. Choosing content that highlights famous people's mistakes, missteps, or other private matters, these videos are sometimes embarrassing.

11. Captured on camera behaving badly, videos show that the constant surveillance that comes with fame can lead to humiliation.

12. Hoping to become famous even for doing something stupid, attention-seeking is one reason for posting videos.

13. Singing, acting, dancing, or performing standup comedy, Internet videos have proven to be an important way to get noticed.

14. Thriving on publicity, viral video fame has also been sought in the realms of politics, advertising, and activism.

15. Sharing video clips with friends, viral videos find a quickly expanding audience.

11.1 Identifying pronouns and antecedents

Identify the pronouns and any antecedents in each of the following sentences, underlining the pronouns once and any antecedents twice. (See *EasyWriter,* Chapter 11.) Example:

> **A guide dog must handle itself well in any situation.**

1. Everyone has seen a guide dog at some time in his or her life.

2. Guide dogs that work with the blind must act as their human partners' eyes.

3. These dogs learn socialization and basic obedience training when they are puppies.

4. Knowing they will have to give up their dog one day, sighted volunteers agree to live with and train a puppy for the first year of its life.

5. Puppies that are destined to be guide dogs are allowed to go into places that routinely refuse entry to other kinds of dogs.

6. If you see a puppy in a supermarket or an office, look for its special coat that identifies it as a trainee guide dog.

7. Volunteer trainers miss their pups after the training period ends, but nothing is more rewarding than knowing that the pups will make life easier for their new owners.

8. Some of the pups do not pass the requirements to become guide dogs, but these are in great demand as household pets.

9. When a dog passes the test and graduates, it and its blind companion learn to work with each other during an intensive training session.

10. If you are interested in learning about guide dogs or in becoming a volunteer, contact your local school for the blind.

11.2 Using subjective-case pronouns

Replace the underlined noun or nouns in each of the following sentences with the appropriate subjective case pronoun. (See *EasyWriter*, 11a.) Example:

$$\text{he}$$
Jack and ~~George~~ visited the new science library.

1. The person who got the highest mark on the test was <u>Susan</u>.

2. Whenever <u>Jerry, David, and Sean</u> went to the beach, the weather was bad.

3. As the sun rose that morning, Melina considered how lucky <u>Melina</u> was to be able to see it.

4. As the cattle crossed the road, <u>the cattle</u> stopped all traffic.

5. Justin, Paolo, and I have a great time whenever <u>Justin, Paolo, and I</u> get together.

6. The library has a collection of Mark Twain's manuscripts, but <u>the manuscripts</u> are not available to the general public.

7. The cars slowed to a stop whenever <u>the cars</u> approached an on-ramp.

8. <u>Tina, Rahul, Fredo, and I</u> stayed up all night watching the complete box set of *The Godfather* on DVD.

9. Fredo decided that <u>Fredo</u> did not like the scene where Michael has his own brother killed.

10. Maya wondered if <u>Maya</u> were smarter than James.

11.3   Using objective-case pronouns

Most of the following sentences use pronouns incorrectly. Revise the incorrect sentences so that they contain correct objective-case pronouns. If a sentence is correct, write C. (See *EasyWriter*, 11a.) Example:

> *me*
> **Eventually, the headwaiter told Kim, Stanley, and ~~I~~ that we could be seated.**

1. Which of the twins are you waiting for—Mary or he?

2. The president gave her the highest praise.

3. Which of those books is for myself?

4. When we asked, the seller promised we that the software would work on a Macintosh computer.

5. Though even the idea of hang gliding made herself nervous, she gave it a try.

6. Max told Jackson and him that the cabin was available to they.

7. Cycling thirty miles a day was triathlon training for Bill, Ubijo, and I.

8. Dennis asked her and me to speak to him in the office.

9. Between you and I, that essay doesn't deserve a high grade.

10. We need two volunteers: yourself and Tom.

11.6 Using pronouns in compound structures, appositives, elliptical clauses; choosing between *we* and *us* before a noun

Choose the appropriate pronoun from the pair in parentheses in each of the following sentences. (See *EasyWriter*, 11a.) Example:

Of the group, only (she/her) and I finished the race.

1. All the other job applicants were far more experienced than (I/me).

2. (We/Us) college students often stay up late.

3. My cousin is much better at skateboarding than (me/I).

4. When their parents retired, (him/he) and his sister took over the family business.

5. The politicians rely on (we/us) citizens to vote.

6. The post-holiday credit card bills were a rude shock to Gary and (she/her).

7. Tomorrow (we/us) Radiohead fans will have an opportunity to purchase concert tickets.

8. The relationship between (they/them) and their brother was often strained.

9. You may think that Anita will win Miss Congeniality, but in fact, everyone likes you better than (she/her).

10. The bride silently fumed, but (she/her) and her maid of honor clearly have different opinions on the dress.

11. Just between you and (I/me), this seminar is a disaster!

12. Staying a week in a lakeside cabin gave (we/us) New Yorkers a much-needed vacation.

13. Lute Johannson always claimed he was the best of (we/us) chili cookers.

14. Jason is younger than (I/me).

15. Seeing (he and I/him and me) dressed up in her best clothes made Mom laugh until she saw the lipstick on the rug.

11.7 **Maintaining pronoun-antecedent agreement**

Revise the following sentences as needed to create pronoun-antecedent agreement and to eliminate the generic *he* and any awkward pronoun references. Some sentences can be revised in more than one way, and two sentences do not require any change. If a sentence is correct as written, write *C*. (See *EasyWriter,* 11b.) Example:

> **Everyone should make his own decision about having children.**
>
> Everyone should make his or her own decision about having children.
> **OR**
> All individuals should make their own decision about having children.

1. Someone who chooses not to have any children of his own is often known today as "child-free" rather than "childless."

2. A child-free person may feel that people with children see his time as less valuable than their own.

3. Corporate culture sometimes offers parents more time off and other perks than it provides to nonparents.

4. A child-free employee may feel that they have to subsidize family medical plans at work for people who have children.

5. Neither parents nor a child-free person has the right to insist that their childbearing choice is the only correct one to make.

6. However, a community has to consider the welfare of their children because caring for and educating children eventually benefits everyone.

7. Neither an educated citizenry nor a skilled workforce can exist if they are not financed and helped by older generations.

8. Almost no one would be able to afford to have children if they were expected to pay for educating and training their offspring entirely without help.

9. People who feel that they should not have to help pay for quality day care and schools have not thought through their responsibilities and needs as members of society.

10. As writer Barbara Kingsolver once pointed out, even someone without children will probably need the services of a doctor or a mechanic in their old age.

11.8 Clarifying pronoun reference

Revise each of the following sentences to clarify pronoun reference. All the items can be revised in more than one way. If a pronoun refers ambiguously to more than one possible antecedent, revise the sentence to reflect each possible meaning. (See *EasyWriter*, 11c.) Example:

> **After Jane left, Miranda found her keys.**
>
> Miranda found Jane's keys after Jane left.
>
> Miranda found her own keys after Jane left.

1. Quint trusted Smith because she had worked for her before.

2. Not long after the company set up the subsidiary, it went bankrupt.

3. When drug therapy is combined with psychotherapy, patients relate better to their therapists, are less vulnerable to what disturbs them, and are more responsive to them.

4. When Deyon was reunited with his father, he wept.

5. Bill happily announced his promotion to Ed.

6. On the weather forecast, it said to expect snow in the overnight hours.

7. The tragedy of child abuse is that even after the children of abusive parents grow up, they often continue the sad tradition of cruelty.

8. Lear divides his kingdom between the two older daughters, Goneril and Regan, whose extravagant professions of love are more flattering than the simple affection of the youngest daughter, Cordelia. The consequences of this error in judgment soon become apparent, as they prove neither grateful nor kind to him.

9. Anna smiled at her mother as she opened the birthday gift.

10. The visit to the pyramids was canceled because of recent terrorist attacks on tourists there, which disappointed Kay, who had waited years to see them.

11.9 Revising to clarify pronoun reference

Revise the following paragraph to establish a clear antecedent for every pronoun that needs one. (See *EasyWriter*, 11c.)

In Paul Fussell's essay "My War," he writes about his experience in combat during World War II, which he says still haunts his life. Fussell confesses that he joined the infantry ROTC in 1939 as a way of getting out of gym class, where he would have been forced to expose his "fat and flabby" body to the ridicule of his classmates. However, it proved to be a serious miscalculation. After the United States entered the war in 1941, other male college students were able to join officer training programs in specialized fields that kept them out of combat. If you were already in an ROTC unit associated with the infantry, though, you were trapped in it. That was how Fussell came to be shipped to France as a rifle-platoon leader in 1944. Almost immediately they sent him to the front, where he soon developed pneumonia because of insufficient winter clothing. He spent a month in hospitals; because he did not want to worry his parents, however, he told them it was just the flu. When he returned to the front, he was wounded by a shell that killed his sergeant.

12.1 Revising comma splices and fused sentences

Revise each of the following comma splices or fused sentences by using the method suggested in brackets after the sentence. (See *EasyWriter*, Chapter 12.) Example:

but
Americans think of slavery as a problem of the past, it still exists in some parts of the world.
      ^
[Join with a comma and a coordinating conjunction.]

1. We tend to think of slavery only in U.S. terms in fact, it began long before the United States existed and still goes on. [Separate into two sentences.]

2. The group Human Rights Watch filed a report on Mauritania, it is a nation in northwest Africa. [Recast as one independent clause.]

3. Slavery has existed in Mauritania for centuries it continues today. [Join with a comma and a coordinating conjunction.]

4. Members of Mauritania's ruling group are called the Beydanes, they are an Arab Berber tribe also known as the White Moors. [Recast as one independent clause.]

5. Another group in Mauritania is known as the Haratin or the Black Moors, they are native West Africans. [Separate into two sentences.]

6. In modern-day Mauritania many of the Haratin are still slaves, they serve the Beydanes. [Join with a semicolon.]

7. The first modern outcry against slavery in Mauritania arose in 1980, protesters objected to the public sale of an enslaved woman. [Recast as an independent and a dependent clause.]

8. Mauritania outlawed slavery in 1981 little has been done to enforce the law. [Join with a comma and a coordinating conjunction.]

9. The law promised slaveholders financial compensation for freeing their slaves however, the language of the law did not explain exactly who would come up with the money. [Join with a semicolon.]

10. Physical force is not usually used to enslave the Haratin, rather, they are held by the force of conditioning. [Separate into two sentences.]

11. In some ways the Mauritanian system is different from slavery in the United States, there are few slave rebellions in Mauritania. [Join with a comma and a coordinating conjunction.]

12. By some estimates 300,000 former slaves still serve their old masters these slaves are psychologically and economically dependent. [Recast as an independent and a dependent clause.]

13. Many Mauritanian slaves live in their own houses, they may work for their former masters in exchange for a home or for food or medical care. [Recast as an independent and a dependent clause.]

14. In addition, there may be as many as 90,000 Haratin still enslaved, some Beydanes have refused to free their slaves unless the government pays compensation. [Join with a semicolon.]

15. Some Mauritanians claim that slavery is not a problem in their country in fact, in 2001, a Mauritanian official told a United Nations committee that slavery had never existed there. [Join with a dash.]

16. Of course, slavery must have existed in Mauritania there would have been no compelling reason to make a decree to abolish it in 1981. [Join with a comma and a coordinating conjunction.]

17. The president of Mauritania insisted in 1997 that discussions of modern slavery were intended only to hurt the country's reputation his comments did not offer much hope for opponents of slavery. [Recast as an independent and a dependent clause.]

18. Both the slaveholding Beydanes and the enslaved Haratin are made up largely of Muslims, some people in Mauritania see resistance to slavery in their country as anti-Muslim. [Join with a comma and a coordinating conjunction.]

19. In some cases, Western opponents of Mauritanian slavery may indeed harbor anti-Muslim sentiments that fact does not justify allowing the slavery to continue. [Join with a semicolon.]

20. Islamic authorities in Mauritania have agreed that all Muslims are equal therefore, one Muslim must not enslave another. [Join with a semicolon.]

12.2 Revising comma splices

Revise the following paragraph, eliminating all comma splices by using a period or a semi-colon. Then revise the paragraph again, this time using any of these three methods:

Separate independent clauses into sentences of their own.

Recast two or more clauses as one independent clause.

Recast one independent clause as a dependent clause.

Comment on the two revisions. What differences in rhythm do you detect? Which version do you prefer, and why? (See *EasyWriter*, Chapter 12.)

My brother, Mark, and I decided to throw a surprise party for our sister's birthday in October, so, we met for lunch at the beginning of September to start brainstorming ideas. Our sister, Vanessa, was turning twenty-one, thus, we wanted the party to be very special. Mark wanted to have the party at our parents' house, I thought it would be more fun to have the party at Vanessa's favorite restaurant, Giorgio's. I explained the reasons that Giorgio's would be better than having the party at home, Mark agreed. I called Giorgio's to reserve space for a private party, meanwhile, Mark mailed invitations to family members and Vanessa's closest friends. Our parents offered to help by pretending to take Vanessa to dinner to celebrate, of course, the plan tricked her perfectly. We were busy the day of the party, we woke up early to prepare. Mark and I spent all afternoon decorating, also, some of Vanessa's friends brought music for the DJ we'd hired. All the guests arrived early, when Vanessa showed up, she was completely surprised! We all enjoyed the delicious food and danced the night away, happily, Vanessa had a wonderful time.

12.3 Revising comma splices and fused sentences

Revise the following paragraph, eliminating the comma splices and fused sentences by using any of these methods:

Separate independent clauses into sentences of their own.

Link clauses with a comma and a coordinating conjunction.

Link clauses with a semicolon and, perhaps, a conjunctive adverb or a transitional phrase.

Recast two or more clauses as one independent clause.

Recast one independent clause as a dependent clause.

Link clauses with a dash.

Then revise the paragraph again, this time eliminating each comma splice and fused sentence by using a different method. Decide which paragraph is more effective, and why. Finally, compare the revision you prefer with the revisions of several other students, and discuss the ways in which the versions differ in meaning. (See *EasyWriter*, Chapter 12.)

When most Americans think of drug dealers, they picture a shadowy figure in a dark alley, there are illicit drug deals in small-town homes and farmhouses, too. A recent survey of young Americans provided evidence that rural teens are more likely than urban ones to use illegal drugs, the young people's drugs of choice include not only marijuana but also methamphetamine and other substances. Meth labs seem to be appearing in more and more small towns these chemical labs are easy and inexpensive to set up in a home or an outbuilding. Methamphetamine addiction is on the rise in rural America, a fact that is devastating to local communities and shocking to those who live elsewhere. Outsiders are likely to forget that rural America is frequently impoverished the teens in poor rural areas are as likely as urban youth to feel bored and trapped in a dead-end existence. Open country and trees are all very well, if there are no jobs, can young people live on bucolic scenery? Many of these teens have seen their parents struggle they cannot really expect their lives to be significantly different. A rural upbringing can't protect children from drugs ensuring that they have hope and constructive ways to spend their time is a much more effective deterrent.

13.1 Eliminating sentence fragments

Revise each of the following fragments, either by combining fragments with independent clauses or by rewriting them as separate sentences. (See *EasyWriter*, Chapter 13.) Example:

> **Zoe looked close to tears. Standing with her head bowed.**
>
> Standing with her head bowed, Zoe looked close to tears.
>
> Zoe looked close to tears. She was standing with her head bowed.

1. Many educators believe students do better in smaller classes. Also, in smaller schools.

2. Her father pulled strings to get her the job. Later regretting his actions.

3. Organized crime has been able to attract graduates just as big business has. With good pay and the best equipment money can buy.

4. Trying to carry a portfolio, art box, illustration boards, and drawing pads. I must have looked ridiculous.

5. The new director made a radical suggestion. That the company should change its name.

6. Stephenie Meyer wrote her young adult novel *Twilight*. After the idea for the book came to her in a dream. She later produced three sequels.

7. The climbers had two choices. To go over a four-hundred-foot cliff or to turn back. They decided to make the attempt.

8. The region has dry, sandy soil. Blown into strange formations by the ever-present wind.

9. The appeal of this film is obvious. Its enthusiastic embrace of sex and violence.

10. To find jobs that can support their families. Many immigrants come to the United States for that reason.

13.2   Revising a paragraph to eliminate sentence fragments

Underline every fragment you find in the following paragraph. Then revise the paragraph. You may combine or rearrange sentences as long as you retain the original content. (See *EasyWriter*, Chapter 13.)

Many of us tell ourselves. "I don't waste electricity. I always turn off the lights when I leave a room." However, many of us waste energy without realizing it. Appliances use a surprising amount of power. Even when they are turned off. Not everyone knows that leaving televisions, computers, and other devices plugged in wastes a lot of electricity. In fact, when we think the stereo is off. It is really only mostly off. Because we use this power without knowing we are using it, often while we are sleeping. People refer to it as "vampire energy" or "phantom power." Fortunately, more and more companies are making electronics and appliances. That have improved power transformers. Allowing the user to leave the device plugged in without wasting more than one watt of electricity. In the meantime, unplugging appliances at night rather than leaving them in standby mode can save energy and money. Sometimes as much as a hundred dollars a year.

13.3 **Understanding intentional fragments**

Choose an advertisement from a newspaper or magazine that contains intentional fragments. Rewrite the advertisement to eliminate all sentence fragments. Be prepared to explain how your version and the original differ in impact and why you think the copywriters for the ad chose to use fragments rather than complete sentences. (See *EasyWriter,* Chapter 13.)

• • • • •

14.1 **Matching subjects and predicates**

Revise each of the following sentences in two ways to make its structures consistent in grammar and meaning. (See *EasyWriter*, 14b.) Example:

> **By studying African American folklore and biblical stories have influenced Toni Morrison's fiction.**
>
> African American folklore and biblical stories have influenced Toni Morrison's fiction.
>
> Toni Morrison's study of African American folklore and biblical stories has influenced her fiction.

1. Toni Morrison's grandmother, who moved to Ohio from the South with only fifteen dollars to her name, and Morrison had great respect for her.

2. In her books, many of which deal with the aftermath of slavery, often feature strong women characters.

3. Published in 1970, Morrison's first novel, *The Bluest Eye*, the story of a young African American girl who wants to look like her Shirley Temple doll.

4. Although Morrison's depictions of African American families and neighborhoods are realistic, but they also include supernatural elements.

5. An important character in Morrison's 1977 novel *Song of Solomon* is about Pilate, a woman with magical powers.

6. *Song of Solomon*, hailed as a masterpiece, winning the National Book Critics Circle Award in 1978.

7. Morrison's fame as a writer won the Pulitzer Prize in fiction in 1988 for *Beloved*.

8. The title character in *Beloved* features the ghost of a murdered infant inhabiting the body of a young woman.

9. When reading *Beloved* makes the horrors of American slavery seem immediate and real.

10. In 1993, Toni Morrison, who became the first African American woman to be awarded the Nobel Prize in literature.

14.2 Making comparisons complete, consistent, and clear

Revise each of the following sentences to eliminate any inappropriate elliptical constructions; to make comparisons complete, logically consistent, and clear; and to supply any other omitted words that are necessary for meaning. (See *EasyWriter*, 14d.) Example:

>   is
> **Most of the candidates are bright, and one brilliant.**
>   ^

1. Our new history professor gives more interesting lectures.

2. Mr. Jones's motorcycle is older than Mr. Murray's and John's.

3. Laws governing drug use in Canada are more liberal than the United States.

4. During spring break, Vanessa decided to visit her family in Canada, Roger decided to travel to Costa Rica, and James to return to his hometown.

5. Argentina and Peru were colonized by Spain, and Brazil by Portugal.

6. The car's exterior is blue, but the seats black vinyl.

7. The house is Victorian, its windows enormous.

8. Are colleges in the United States as competitive or more competitive than they were five years ago?

9. My new stepmother makes my father happier.

10. She argued that children are even more important for men than women.

14.3 Revising for consistency and completeness

Revise this passage so that all sentences are grammatically and logically consistent and complete. (See *EasyWriter*, Chapter 14.)

A concentrated animal feeding operation, or CAFO, is when a factory farm raises thousands of animals in a confined space. Vast amounts of factory-farm livestock waste, dumped into giant lagoons, which are an increasingly common sight in rural areas of this country. Are factory-farm operations healthy for their neighbors, for people in other parts of the country, and the environment? Many people think that these operations damage our air and water more than small family farms.

One problem with factory farming is the groundwater in the Midwest that has been contaminated by toxic waste. In addition, air quality produces bad-smelling and sometimes dangerous gases that people living near a CAFO have to breathe. When a factory farm's neighbors complain may not be able to close the operation. The reason is because most factory farms have powerful corporate backers.

Not everyone is angry about the CAFO situation; consumers get a short-term benefit from a large supply of pork, beef, and chicken that is cheaper than family farms can raise. However, the more people know about factory farms, the less interest in supporting their farming practices.

15.1 Identifying conjunctions

Underline the coordinating and subordinating conjunctions as well as the conjunctive adverbs in each of the following sentences. (See *EasyWriter*, Chapter 15.) Example:

> **We used sleeping bags <u>even though</u> the cabin had both sheets <u>and</u> blankets.**

1. He couldn't decide whether to go skiing as usual or to try snowboarding.

2. We shopped for a sweater for my grandmother and a hat for my grandfather while Mom selected some ties for Dad.

3. Pokey is an outside cat; nevertheless, she greets me at the front door each night as I arrive home.

4. When we arrived at the pond, we saw many children playing there.

5. Although I live in a big city, my neighborhood has enough trees and raccoons to make me feel as though I live in the suburbs.

6. Ambitious men and women worked on the campaign until the early hours of the morning.

7. Because the downtown area has many successful businesses, people still want to live inside the city limits.

15.2 Combining sentences with coordination

Using the principles of coordination to signal equal importance or to create special emphasis, combine and revise the following twelve short sentences into several longer and more effective ones. Add or delete words as necessary. (See *EasyWriter*, Chapter 15.)

The bull-riding arena was fairly crowded. The crowd made no impression on me. I had made a decision. It was now time to prove myself. I was scared. I walked to the entry window. I placed my money on the counter. The clerk held up a Stetson hat filled with slips of paper. I reached in. I picked one. The slip held the number of the bull I was to ride. I headed toward the stock corral.

15.3 Writing sentences with subordination

Combine each of the following sets of sentences into one sentence that uses subordination to signal the relationships among ideas. Add or delete words as necessary. (See *EasyWriter*, 15b.) Example:

The bus swerved to avoid hitting a dog.

It narrowly missed a car.

The car was in the bus driver's blind spot.

When the bus swerved to avoid hitting a dog, it narrowly missed a car that was in the bus driver's blind spot.

1. The scenery in the park is beautiful.

   The mountains have caps of snow.

   The lakes are deep and full of fish.

   The pastures are green.

   It is an ideal spot to spend spring break.

2. I spent a long night on a sleep sofa.

   I was at my parents' house.

   The sleep sofa has an uncomfortably thin mattress with a hard metal bar beneath it.

3. Al Franken wrote a book about conservatives in American media.

   Fox News filed a lawsuit to stop publication of the book.

   The lawsuit was thrown out of court.

   The book became a best seller.

4. I walked into the shelter.

   Men, women, and children were slumped against the wall.

   Shopping carts containing families' belongings lay on their sides.

5. We had dug a seventy-foot ditch.

   My boss would pour gravel into the ditch.

   I would level the gravel with a shovel.

15.4 Using coordination and subordination

Revise the following paragraph, using coordination and subordination where appropriate to clarify the relationships between ideas. (See *EasyWriter*, Chapter 15.)

Samosas are small, crispy pastries. They are usually deep-fried. The pastry shells are often triangular. They are stuffed with an assortment of spiced fillings. One type of filling is minced meat. Vegetable fillings may be potatoes, cauliflower, onions, or peas. It is also common to stuff a samosa with dried fruits and nuts. Samosas are a common snack in Asia, Africa, and the Arabian Peninsula. Samosas are especially popular in India. However, the snack did not originate in India. Traders from Central Asia probably brought samosas to India. The pastries were easy to make and to pack on a long journey. Today, people often enjoy a samosa with a cup of chai.

16.1 **Eliminating unnecessary words and phrases**

Make each of the following sentences clear and concise by eliminating unnecessary words and phrases and by making additions or revisions as needed. (See *EasyWriter*, Chapter 16.) Example:

> The ~~incredible, unbelievable~~ feats that Houdini performed amazed ~~and astounded~~ all of his audiences ~~who came to see him.~~

1. Harry Houdini, whose real birth name was Ehrich Weiss, made the claim that he had been born in Appleton, Wisconsin, but in actual fact he was born into the world in Budapest, Hungary.

2. Shortly after Houdini's birth, his family moved to Appleton, where his father served as the one and only rabbi in Appleton at that point in time.

3. Houdini gained fame as a really great master escape artist.

4. His many numerous escapes included getting out of a giant sealed envelope without tearing it and walking out of jail cells that were said to be supposedly escape-proof.

5. Before his untimely early death, Houdini told his brother to burn and destroy all papers describing how Houdini's illusions worked.

6. Clearly, it is quite obvious that Houdini did not want anyone at all to know his hidden secrets.

7. Part of the explanation for Houdini's escape artistry lies in the fact that his physique was in absolutely peak physical condition.

8. Houdini's tremendous control over almost every single individual muscle allowed him to contort his body into seemingly impossible positions.

9. After his mother's death, Houdini grew interested in spiritualism until he discovered that the mediums who were the people running the séances were frauds trying to do nothing more than bilk and cheat their customers.

10. On his deathbed, Houdini promised his wife that he would try and attempt to make contact with her from beyond the grave, but so far, he has never been able to get in touch yet.

16.2   Revising for conciseness

Revise the following paragraph so that each sentence is as concise as possible. Combine or divide sentences if necessary. (See *EasyWriter*, Chapter 16.)

Currently, Chinese pianist Lang Lang is one of the most talked about and discussed musicians playing classical music today. The reason is because this young man has accomplished a lot of things in his few short years. He has played all over the world with many of the world's most famous and well-known orchestras, and it is a fact that he has recorded several immensely popular CDs. In 2008, Lang Lang performed at the opening ceremony of the Beijing Olympics and at Macy's Thanksgiving Day parade in New York City. Both of these televised events were broadcast all around the entire world, and people all over the map got to see him play. He is, however, a somewhat controversial figure, provoking disagreements among his listeners. His performing style when he is playing in front of a live audience has been described by critics as excessive and overdone. Some music reviewers disapprove of the way in which he chooses to interpret music written by classical composers. His fans, however, enjoy their beloved pianist and his style and way of playing, which they see as energetic and full of life. Ultimately, it is agreed upon that, whatever one thinks of his approach, Lang Lang has great talent and wide-reaching ambition.

17.1 **Creating parallel words or phrases**

Complete the following sentences, using parallel words or phrases in each case. (See *Easy-Writer*, Chapter 17.) Example:

    The wise politician <u>promises the possible</u> , <u>effects the unavoidable</u> , **and**

    <u>accepts the inevitable</u> .

1. My favorite pastimes include _____ , _____ , and _____ .

2. I want not only _____ but also _____ .

3. My motto is _____ , _____ , and _____ .

4. I told my younger sister _____ and _____ .

5. _____ , _____ , and _____ are chores I did as a teenager.

6. When he got his promotion, he _____ , _____ , and _____ .

7. You should _____ , _____ , and _____ before opening your own restaurant.

8. We must either _____ or _____ .

9. Graduates find that the job market _____ , _____ , and _____ .

10. A good leader must _____ and _____ .

17.2 Revising sentences for parallelism

Revise the following sentences to eliminate any errors in parallel structure. (See *EasyWriter*, Chapter 17.) Example:

> Pérez Prado's orchestra was famous for playing irresistible rhythms and ~~because it turned~~ ^{turning} the mambo into a new dance craze.

1. The latest dance steps and wearing festive party clothes were necessities for many teenagers in the 1950s.

2. Many people in this country remember how they danced to the mambo music of the 1950s and listening to that era's Latin bands.

3. Older dancers may recall Rosemary Clooney, Perry Como, and Ruth Brown singing mambo numbers and Pérez Prado's band had a huge hit, "Cherry Pink and Apple Blossom White."

4. Growing up near Havana and a student of classical piano, Pérez Prado loved Cuban music.

5. Pérez Prado wanted not only to play Cuban music but also he wanted to combine it with elements of jazz.

6. Playing piano in Havana nightclubs, arranging music for a Latin big band, and the jam sessions he joined with the band's guitarists gave him the idea for a new kind of music.

7. The result was a new dance phenomenon: mambo music was born, and Pérez Prado, who became known as "King of the Mambo."

8. Prado conducted his orchestra with hand-waving, head and shoulder movements, and by kicking his feet high in the air.

9. His recordings feature syncopated percussion, wailing trumpets, and Prado shouted rhythmically.

10. Pérez Prado, innovative and a great musician, died in 1989.

17.3 Revising for parallelism and supplying necessary words

Revise the following paragraph to maintain parallelism where it exists and to supply all words necessary for clarity, grammar, and idiom in parallel structures. (See *EasyWriter*, Chapter 17.)

Family gatherings for events such as weddings, holidays, and going on vacation are supposed to be happy occasions, but for many people, getting together with family members causes tremendous stress. Everyone hopes to share warm memories and for a picture-perfect family event. Unfortunately, the reality may include an uncle who makes offensive remarks, a critical mother, or anger at a spouse who doesn't lift a finger to help. Neither difficult relatives nor when things go wrong will necessarily ruin a big family gathering, however. The trick is to plan for problems and being able to adapt. Family members who are not flexible, not pleasant to be around, or willing to do their part will always be a problem for their relatives. However, people who try to make a family gathering a success will almost always either be able to enjoy the event or laugh about it later.

18.1   Revising for verb tense and mood

Revise any of the following sentences in which you find unnecessary shifts in verb tense or in mood. If a sentence is correct as written, write C. (See *EasyWriter*, Chapter 18.) Examples:

> *spend*
> When the weather is good, the children ~~spent~~ at least four hours a week playing soccer in the park.

> Write a letter to your local representatives requesting more parks, and ~~you should~~ ask your neighbors to sign it.

1. In the eighteenth century, Romantic poets believed that nature can help individuals find their true selves.

2. Today, many people still go into nature when they needed to do some soul-searching.

3. However, there are also very practical reasons to head outdoors. People now know that spending time in nature was good for their health.

4. Studies showed that being in a natural setting helps reduce people's stress levels.

5. Recently, researchers discover that if children spend time in green spaces on a regular basis, they are less likely to become obese.

6. Take your children to the park frequently, and you will see the difference for yourself.

7. Pay attention to the study that indicates that taking walks in nature helps children with attention deficit hyperactivity disorder (ADHD).

8. In this study, the children who take walks in green spaces showed an improved ability to concentrate.

9. Perhaps if all children spent several hours a week playing outside, fewer of them suffer from ADHD.

10. Learn to incorporate outdoor activities into your daily life because fresh air and sunlight are good for everyone, not just children.

18.2 **Eliminating shifts in voice and point of view**

Revise each of the following sentences to eliminate an unnecessary shift in voice or point of view. (See *EasyWriter*, 18b–c.) Example:

> fiddler played a
> **The dancers performed on a low stage as a jig ~~was played by a fiddler~~.**
> ⌃

1. We can make a difference in the community if you find time to volunteer each week.

2. The painters covered the furniture with drop cloths and the floors were protected with plastic sheets.

3. You should always pursue your dreams, even if one meets challenges along the way.

4. When someone says "roommate" to a high school senior bound for college, thoughts of no privacy and potential fights are conjured up.

5. The physician moves the knee around to observe the connections of the cartilage and ligaments, and a fluid is injected into the joint.

6. We knew that you shouldn't walk across the railroad trestle, but we went ahead anyway.

7. When the snapping turtle attacked Jake and me, Jake was bitten on the hand, but I swam away.

8. The roses were gathered by Lionel, and then he arranged them.

9. Sea anemones thrive in coastal tide pools, but it cannot survive outside the water for very long.

10. Suddenly we heard an explosion of wings off to our right, and you could see a hundred or more ducks lifting off from the water.

18.3 **Eliminating shifts between direct and indirect discourse**

To eliminate the shifts between direct and indirect discourse in the following sentences, put the direct discourse into indirect form. (See *EasyWriter*, 18d.) Example:

> states   his
> **Steven Pinker ~~stated~~ that ~~my~~ book is meant for people who use language and respect it.**

1. Richard Rodriguez acknowledges that intimacy is not created by a language; "it is created by intimates."

2. She said that during a semester abroad, "I really missed all my friends."

3. The bewildered neighbor asked him, "What the heck he thought he was doing on the roof?"

4. Loren Eiseley feels an urge to join the birds in their soundless flight, but in the end he understands that he cannot, and "I was, after all, only a man."

5. The instructor told us, "Please read the next two stories before the next class" and that she might give us a quiz on them.

18.4 Eliminating shifts in tone and diction

Revise each of the following sentences to eliminate shifts in tone and diction. (See *EasyWriter*, 18e.) Example:

How do I
Excuse me. ~~In which direction should I proceed to~~ **get to the mall?**

1. I am astounded by the number of emails I receive each day trying to flog meds to me.

2. The Chinese invented noodles, though lots of people think that the Italians must have come up with that bright idea.

3. Most commuters keep to a predictable schedule, hopping a bus or train to the 'burbs at the same time each night.

4. Many activists try to publicize their cause by bullying innocent pedestrians who are minding their own business.

5. The moment I walked into the furniture store, the proprietor of the establishment endeavored to sell me a couch.

• • • • •

19.1 Using a comma to set off introductory elements

In the following sentences, add any commas that are needed after the introductory element. If no comma is necessary, write C. (See *EasyWriter*, 19a.) Example:

Using technology in new ways, scientists are working on an electronic nose.

1. Although the idea of an electronic nose may sound odd such a nose would have many uses.

2. In the past doctors recognized some ailments by a characteristic odor.

3. Having strep throat causes a person to give off a particular scent that a trained nose can identify.

4. Of course throat cultures can also spot strep throat, but they take time.

5. When a strep infection is identified immediately by its smell a patient can get immediate treatment.

6. Someday electronic noses may be perfected.

7. Along with this technological advance is likely to come disbelief that electronic noses could be useful.

8. Naturally people may appreciate the idea of using electronic noses to avoid invasive medical procedures.

9. If electronic noses become more sensitive they could be used for tasks human noses find unpleasant.

10. Unable to judge whether smells are delectable or nauseating an electronic nose might be a valuable aid to a human one.

19.2 Using a comma in compound sentences

Use a comma and a coordinating conjunction (*and, but, or, for, nor, so,* or *yet*) to combine each of the following pairs of sentences into one sentence. Delete or rearrange words if necessary. (See *EasyWriter,* 19b.) Example:

> **The phrase *test-tube baby* is rarely used today, yet In vitro fertilization is common.**

1. Treatments for infertility become more promising each year. In vitro fertilization has helped many people have children.

2. Over two decades ago, fertility treatments were a little-explored field. The first "test-tube baby" astonished the world.

3. *In vitro* means "in glass." In vitro fertilization does indeed take place in a lab dish.

4. A scientist combines an egg cell and a sperm cell. An embryo forms when the egg cell begins to divide.

5. The embryo that grows is returned to the mother's uterus. The process of growing to viability cannot take place entirely in a laboratory.

6. The procedure requires scientific intervention. The parents of a "test-tube baby" have a child that is biologically theirs.

7. Before in vitro fertilization, would-be parents might have given up on the idea of having children. They might have spent years trying to adopt a child.

8. In vitro fertilization has helped many people have children. It is expensive.

9. There are other, newer methods of helping infertile couples. In vitro fertilization no longer astonishes the public.

10. The first "test-tube baby," who was born in England, was a celebrity. Today, children whose parents used in vitro fertilization are quite common.

19.3 **Recognizing restrictive and nonrestrictive elements**

First, underline the restrictive or the nonrestrictive elements in the following sentences. Then, use commas to set off the nonrestrictive elements in any of the sentences that contain such elements. (See *EasyWriter*, 19c.) Example:

> **My only novel, *The Family Kurasch*, is out of print.**

1. Anyone who is fourteen years old faces strong peer pressure every day.

2. A person who suffers from asthma must avoid dust and sometimes exercise to prevent asthma attacks.

3. Nutritious foods such as fruits and vegetables give people more energy.

4. Arthur Miller's play *Death of a Salesman* won the Pulitzer Prize.

5. The president elected for a six-year term acts as head of state.

6. Thurgood Marshall the first African American to serve on the U.S. Supreme Court died in 1993.

7. Houses made of wood can often survive earthquakes.

8. Steve Jobs and Steve Wozniak the founders of Apple Computer invented the personal computer.

9. The man who rescued her puppy won her eternal gratitude.

10. The tornado which had spared Waterville leveled Douglastown.

19.4 Using commas to set off items in a series

In the following sentences, add any commas that are needed to set off words, phrases, or clauses in a series. If no comma is needed, write C. (See *EasyWriter*, 19d.) Example:

The waiter brought water, menus, and an attitude.

1. From his new job, Jake wanted money prestige and a challenge, in that order.

2. I am looking forward to turning eighteen being able to vote and perhaps serving in the military.

3. The spider's orange body resembles a colored dot amidst eight long black legs.

4. The moon circles the earth the earth revolves around the sun and the sun is just one star among many in the Milky Way galaxy.

5. The theater troupe spent weeks memorizing lines rehearsing scenes and building sets.

6. After the music festival, Ariana collected countless plastic bottles from the lawn.

7. Whether in the field at the office or on a lecture tour scientist Tim Flannery excels at his work.

8. The firm's quiet pleasant excessively polite public relations executives made everyone a little nervous.

9. James Joyce wrote novels short stories and poems.

10. The orientation packet for visiting students outlined the essentials: what to bring what to expect where to go on the first day.

19.5 Using commas to set off parenthetical and transitional expressions, contrasting elements, interjections, direct address, and tag questions

Revise each of the following sentences, using commas to set off parenthetical and transitional expressions, contrasting elements, interjections, words used in direct address, and tag questions. (See *EasyWriter*, 19f.) Example:

> Ladies and gentlemen, thank you for your attention.

1. The choice is of course entirely up to you.

2. However we believe that democracy is the most effective form of government.

3. Now we can stitch the seam right?

4. You've studied the formulas for the math test haven't you?

5. Nurse do I need another vaccination today?

6. Captain Kirk I'm a doctor not a madman.

7. The celebration will alas conclude all too soon.

8. One must consider the society as a whole not just its parts.

9. Her friends did not know about her illness did they?

10. Mary announced, "Kids I want you to clean your rooms not make a bigger mess."

19.6 Using commas with dates, addresses, and quotations

Revise each of the following sentences, using commas appropriately with dates, addresses and place-names, and quotations. If no comma is needed in a sentence, write C. (See *Easy-Writer*, 19g–h.) Example:

> Before December 23, 2008, the Janesville Assembly Plant was located at 1000 General Motors
> ^
> Drive, Janesville, Wisconsin.
>   ^   ^

1. James Baldwin wrote in 1953 "This world is white no longer, and it will never be white again."

2. Who remarked that "youth is wasted on the young"?

3. "The public be damned!" William Henry Vanderbilt was reported to have said. "I'm working for my stockholders."

4. "Who can match the desperate humorlessness of the adolescent who thinks he is the first to discover seriousness?", asks P. J. Kavanaugh.

5. Teach For America's national office is at 315 West Thirty-sixth Street Seventh Floor New York New York 10018.

6. The ship was hit by two torpedoes on May 7 1915 and sank in minutes.

7. "Hip-hop culture is probably one of the most powerful things to come out of America in a long time" according to musician will.i.am.

19.7 **Eliminating unnecessary and inappropriate commas**

Revise each of the following sentences, deleting unnecessary commas. If a sentence contains no unnecessary commas, write C. (See *EasyWriter*, 19i.) Example:

> **Insomniacs are people, who have a hard time sleeping soundly.**

1. Contrary to popular belief, insomnia is not simply a matter, of being unable to sleep well at night.

2. Insomniacs do indeed wake up at night, but, studies have demonstrated that they also have trouble napping during the day.

3. Why can't insomniacs sleep soundly at night, or nap when they are tired?

4. In many cases, insomniacs suffer, from anxiety.

5. Doctors and sleep researchers, have long considered anxiety to be a common result of getting too little sleep.

6. However, recent studies indicate that anxiety contributes to sleeplessness, not the other way around.

7. Therapies to help insomniacs, include behavior modification and sleeping pills.

8. Sleep therapists recommend, going to bed at the same time every night, not watching television in bed, and not reading in bed.

9. Restless, disturbed, sleep habits are certainly irritating, but are they also, bad for an insomniac's health?

10. Although tired people are more dangerous drivers, and less productive workers, no one knows for certain, if insomnia can actually make them sick.

20.1 Using semicolons to link clauses

Combine each of the following pairs of sentences into one sentence by using a semicolon. (See *EasyWriter*, 20a–b.) Example:

                              ; meet
Take the bus to Henderson Street. ~~Meet~~ me under the clock.

1. Veterans Day honors American military veterans. It was originally called Armistice Day, a day set aside to honor veterans of World War I.

2. Pilates exercise includes specific strength and balance exercises combined with focused breathing patterns. As a result, people experience increased lung capacity, better circulation, and improved strength, flexibility, and balance.

3. Voltaire was concerned about the political implications of his skepticism. He warned his friends not to discuss atheism in front of the servants.

4. The unwanted package arrived C.O.D. I politely refused to pay the charges.

5. Current celebrities don't have to make fools of themselves on reality television shows. Former celebrities jump at the chance.

6. Pittsburgh was once notorious for its smoke and grime. Today, its skies and streets are cleaner than those of many other American cities.

7. I used to see nothing but woods when I looked out my back window. The view was nothing like it is now, a treeless expanse of new houses.

8. Establishing your position in an office is an important task. Your profile will mold your relationships with other staff members.

9. Teresa has a fear of public speaking. Therefore, she dislikes giving class presentations.

10. Florida's mild winter climate is ideal for bicycling. In addition, the terrain is very flat.

20.2   **Eliminating misused semicolons**

Revise each of the following sentences to correct the misuse of semicolons. (See *EasyWriter,* 20d.) Example:

> **The new system would encourage high school students to take more academic courses;,**
>
>   **^**
>
> **thus strengthening college preparation.**

1.   We must find a plan to provide decent health care; a necessity in today's life.

2.   Mei Ching was born in the Year of the Horse; while her sister was born in the Year of the Rooster.

3.   For four glorious but underpaid weeks this summer; I'll be working in Yosemite.

4.   Finally, I found her at the Humane Society; a beautiful shepherd-collie mix who likes children and plays well with cats.

5.   If the North had followed up its victory at Gettysburg more vigorously; the Civil War might have ended sooner.

6.   He left a large estate; which was used to endow a scholarship fund.

7.   For many people, saving money means; sharing an apartment, eating at home, and not owning a car.

8.   Working full-time and going to school is not always possible; despite what some people may tell you.

9.   After school; many fourteen-year-olds head to the mall; where they spend the rest of the day.

10.   The speech made sense to some observers; but not to me.

21.1 Using periods appropriately

Revise each of the following sentences, inserting periods in the appropriate places and eliminating any inappropriate punctuation. If a sentence is correct, write C. (See *EasyWriter*, 21a.) Example:

Ban Ki-moon became secretary-general of the United Nations in 2007⊙

1. According to the organization's charter, the secretary-general is the UN's "chief administrative officer".

2. The appointment of Ban Ki-moon to a powerful leadership position surprised some people!

3. The Korean diplomat won approval by visiting each of the fifteen countries in the UN Security Council and proving he was right for the job

4. Though he does not have a PhD., he has decades of experience in international relations and knows five languages.

5. Before he became secretary-general, Mr. Ban served as a diplomat and spent several years working in Washington, DC

6. He has a reputation for being a hard worker who does not think twice about starting his workday at 5:00 a.m..

7. As secretary-general, he has seriously questioned whether humans are doing enough to combat global warming?

8. Mr Ban stresses the importance of this issue in his conversations with world leaders.

9. However, global warming is only one of many challenges he faces as leader of this international organization.

10. Preserving human rights and working for peace worldwide are also part of the job!

21.2 Using question marks appropriately

Revise each of the following sentences, adding question marks, substituting question marks for other punctuation where appropriate, and removing inappropriately placed question marks. Some sentences do not require any question marks; for those sentences, write *C*. (See *EasyWriter*, 21b.) Example:

> **She asked the travel agent, "What is the airfare to Greece?"**

1. We asked the meteorologist what types of clouds indicate rain?

2. "Is this the best route to the museum," Olivia asked the cab driver.

3. Did you just say, "What time is it?"?

4. "How long are we supposed to wait for Sara," wondered Erin?

5. Who said, "A penny saved is a penny earned"?

6. She asked the officer if she could call her lawyer.

7. "Have you heard the one about the tourist and the barber," he asked.

8. What do you think of your classes? Your professors?

21.3 Using exclamation points appropriately

Revise each of the following sentences, adding or deleting exclamation points as necessary and removing any other inappropriate punctuation that you find. (See *EasyWriter*, 21c.) Example:

Look out͵ the tide is coming in fast͵!

1. The defendant stood up in the witness box and shouted, "I didn't do it. You've got to believe me."

2. That's amazing. He's broken the world record.

3. The child cried, "Ouch" as her mother pulled off the bandage!

4. "Go! Go! Go!," roared the crowd as the quarterback sped toward the end zone.

5. "I don't believe it," she gasped when I told her she'd won the election!

22.1 Using apostrophes to signal possession

Complete each of the following sentences by inserting 's or just an apostrophe to form the possessive case of the italicized words. (See *EasyWriter*, 22a.) Example:

> For years, I relied on my *parents'* cooking and my favorite Chinese *restaurant's* delivery.

1. When I told my best *friends* boyfriend that I've been learning how to cook, he just laughed.

2. *Lindsays* boyfriend, Evan, is a sous chef at one of *Bostons* trendiest restaurants.

3. My *friends* excited responses to my cooking declaration were encouraging.

4. *Evan* ears perked, however, when I told him I'd been reading cookbooks and watching cooking shows.

5. The first recipe I tried came from Nigel Slater's *Appetite*, a cookbook I borrowed from the library.

6. Although I want to have my own cookbook collection one day, my local *library* cooking section is impressive.

7. So until I start to feel comfortable following recipes, I will use the *Internet* resources and my library card.

8. The fancy kitchen store near my apartment carries all sorts of amateur and advanced home *cooks* tools.

9. Eventually, I want to purchase a *chef* knife and a cast iron pot.

10. Even though I'm a novice at the stove, I agree with Evan that most *dishes* success lies in the power of their ingredients.

22.2 Using apostrophes appropriately

Revise each of the following sentences so that it uses apostrophes appropriately. (See *Easy-Writer*, 22a.) Example:

> That's
> ~~Thats~~ the classical music used in the movie *Elvira Madigan*.
>   ^

1. She is his favorite person, but he is not her's.

2. Please ask where were going so we do'nt get lost.

3. Your going to be late for your nine oclock appointment.

4. That guy whose been giving you a ride after work called at about nine o'clock.

5. For the test youll be taking on Monday, youre required to have a No. 2 pencil.

6. The bike Im riding to school is'nt new, but its in good shape.

7. The caller says he has been waiting an hour for his pizza's, but we don't have any record of his order.

8. The distributor says that your order has not received it's approval from the business office.

9. It's true that a snake can shed it's own skin and can swallow much of its prey whole.

10. That cat of your's is nothing but trouble.

23.1 Using quotation marks to signal direct quotation

In the following sentences, add quotation marks each time someone else's exact words are being used. Some sentences do not require quotation marks; mark correct sentences *C*. (See *EasyWriter*, 23a.) Example:

"Your phone's ringing!" yelled Phil from the end of the hall.

1. Although many people believe that Rick says, Play it again, Sam, in *Casablanca*, those exact words do not appear in the film.

2. After a tornado ripped through her house, a tearful Indiana woman said she had nothing left.

3. Researchers recently stated that infants who are exposed to peanuts have a reduced risk of developing a peanut allergy later in life.

4. Yesterday, the president told Congress, Democrats and Republicans need to cooperate.

5. Call me Ishmael is the first sentence of novelist Herman Melville's *Moby Dick*.

6. Most people like to think of themselves as open-minded and flexible enough to change when the circumstances demand.

7. After repeating I can't hear you with her fingers stuck in her ears, Hannah ran to her room and slammed the door.

8. Ours is the most imaginative generation in recent history, he wrote.

9. Keep your opinions to yourselves, Dad muttered as he served the lumpy oatmeal.

10. Is the computer plugged in? the technical support operator asked, prompting Harry to snarl, Yes, I'm not a complete idiot.

23.2 Using quotation marks for titles and definitions

Revise each of the following sentences, using quotation marks appropriately to signal titles and definitions. (See *EasyWriter*, 23b.) Example:

> **The Chinese American businessman surprised his guest by using the Hebrew word *shalom*, which means "peace."**

1. John Lennon wrote the song Imagine after he left the Beatles.

2. My dictionary defines *isolation* as the quality or state of being alone.

3. The *Friday Night Lights* episode The Giving Tree received both praise and criticism.

4. Kowinski uses the term *mallaise* to mean physical and psychological disturbances caused by mall contact.

5. The film is based on the short story The Curious Case of Benjamin Button by F. Scott Fitzgerald.

6. "The little that is known about gorillas certainly makes you want to know more," writes Alan Moorehead in his essay A Most Forgiving Ape.

7. The British, the guide told us, knit sweaters for their teapots.

8. If you had ever had Stairway to Heaven running through your head for four days straight, you would not like Led Zeppelin either.

9. Big Bill, a section of Dos Passos's book *U.S.A.*, opens with a birth.

10. Amy Lowell challenges social conformity in her poem Patterns.

23.3 Using quotation marks appropriately

Revise each of the following sentences, deleting quotation marks used inappropriately, moving those placed incorrectly, and changing wording as necessary. (See *EasyWriter*, Chapter 23.) Example:

Do advertisements ⸌really⸍ have something to teach us about our culture?

1. Cable channels such as "Nickelodeon" include what they term "classic" commercials as part of the programming.

2. Television commercials have frequently used "popular" songs as an effective way to connect their product with good feelings in consumers' minds.

3. Many middle-aged Americans still associate the wee-oo sound of the theremin from the Beach Boys' Good Vibrations with images of beachgoers enjoying orange soft drinks.

4. The strategy of using hit songs in commercials can "backfire" when the listeners don't like the song or like it too much to think of it as an advertising "jingle."

5. Many aging baby boomers were disturbed to hear "Beatles" songs being used to sell shoes.

6. The rights to many Beatles songs, such as "Revolution", are no longer controlled by the Beatles.

7. Sometimes advertisements contain songs that seem to have no connection at all to the products being "plugged."

8. Many Iggy Pop fans wonder what on earth his song Lust for Life has to do with taking an expensive ocean cruise.

9. Not surprisingly, the song's more peculiar lyrics, including Well, that's like hypnotizing chickens, are omitted from the cruise-line advertisements.

10. Do consumers love the songs of their youth so much that merely hearing a song in an "ad" will make them buy that car?

24.1 Using parentheses and brackets

Revise the following sentences, using parentheses and brackets correctly. Change any other punctuation in the sentences as needed. (See *EasyWriter*, 24a–b.) Example:

               (   )

For years, people both scientists and nonscientists have argued about how much influence
                   ^   ^

birth order has on our personalities.

1. Do we turn out differently depending on our birth order for instance, only child, oldest child, middle child, or youngest child?

2. Generally, most acknowledge that firstborn children (including only children show a greater sense of responsibility and self-confidence.

3. Later-born children, (those with at least one older sibling,) tend to take more risks and have lower self-esteem.

4. However, experts have not yet proven [through reliable scientific studies, that is] that these generalizations are true.

5. Nevertheless, researchers who study birth order have been able to identify a few interesting patterns (some of which are quite surprising.)

6. Initial studies indicate that middle children may have an increased risk of developing certain health problems (including depression and chronic fatigue syndrome (CFS)).

7. Also, according to a study in *Science* magazine, (a well-respected scientific journal) firstborn children tend to have higher IQs.

8. However, this conclusion like most claims relating to birth order, has been questioned.

9. After analyzing data from the National Longitudinal Survey of Youth [NLSY], one group concluded that no correlation exists between birth order and intelligence.

10. Clearly, more research is needed if we want to resolve the "contradictory findings and long-standing conceptual disagreements" that characterize the debate about birth order and intelligence, Sulloway 1711.

24.2 Using dashes

Revise the following sentences so that dashes are used correctly. If the sentence is correct as written, write C. (See *EasyWriter,* 24c.) Example:

In some states‾California, for example‾banks are no longer allowed to charge ATM users an

additional fee for withdrawing money.

1. Many consumers accept the fact that they have to pay additional fees for services such as bank machines if they don't want to pay, they don't have to use the service.

2. Nevertheless,—extra charges seem to be added to more and more services all the time.

3. Some of the charges are ridiculous why should hotels charge guests a fee for making a toll-free telephone call?

4. The hidden costs of service fees are irritating people feel that their bank accounts are being nibbled to death.

5. But some of the fees consumers are asked to pay—are more than simply irritating.

6. The "convenience charges" — that people have to pay when buying show tickets by telephone — are often a substantial percentage of the cost of the ticket.

7. If ticket buyers don't want to pay these "convenience charges" and who does? they must buy their tickets at the box office.

8. Finally, there are government fees that telephone companies and other large corporations are required to pay.

9. Telephone companies routinely pass these fees used to ensure Internet access to remote areas and schools along to their customers, implying that the government expects consumers to pay.

10. Many consumers are not aware that the government requires the corporations—not the general public—to pay these fees.

24.3 Using colons

Insert a colon in each of the following items that needs one. If the sentence is correct as written, write *C*. (See *EasyWriter*, 24d.) Example:

> **Some fans of the *Star Wars* films have created a new online version of *Episode I: The Phantom Menace* that deletes all of the scenes with Jar Jar Binks.**

1. Gandhi urged four rules tell the truth even in business, adopt more sanitary habits, abolish caste and religious divisions, and learn English.

2. Solid vocal technique is founded on the correct use of head position, diaphragm control, muscle relaxation, and voice placement.

3. Another example is taken from Psalm 139 16.

4. The sonnet's structure is effective in revealing the speaker's message love has changed his life and ended his depression.

5. The article "The Science of Romance Why We Flirt" suggests that both married and single people flirt but for different reasons.

6. The filmmakers clearly knew what the audience wanted adventure, suspense, and romance.

7. Voters rejected the school budget increase by a 2,1 margin, leaving school officials wondering how to cope with classroom overcrowding.

8. Education can alleviate problems such as poverty, poor health, and the energy shortage.

9. The interviewer asked each of the applicants the same question "Why do you want to go to medical school?"

10. Every week, my father watches his favorite television shows *The Office, Lost*, and *Dancing with the Stars*.

24.4   Using ellipses

Read the following passage. Then assume that the underlined portions have been left out in a reprinting of the passage. Indicate how you would use ellipses to indicate those deletions. (See *EasyWriter*, 24f.) Example:

> Saving money is difficult ~~for young people in entry-level positions~~, but it is important.
>   . . .

Should young people <u>who are just getting started in their careers</u> think about saving for retirement? Those who begin to save in their twenties <u>are making a wise financial decision. They</u> are putting away money that can earn compound interest for decades. Even if they save only a hundred dollars a month, and even if they stop saving when they hit age thirty-five, the total forty years later will be impressive. <u>On the other hand,</u> people who wait until they are fifty to begin saving will have far less money put aside at the age of sixty-five. People who wait too long may face an impoverished retirement <u>unless they are able to save thousands of dollars each month</u>. Of course, no one knows how long he or she will live, but saving is a way of gambling on reaching retirement. Difficult as it may be to think about being sixty-five or seventy years old, young people should plan ahead.

24.5 Reviewing punctuation marks

Correct the punctuation in the following sentences. If the punctuation is correct as written, write *C*. (See *EasyWriter*, Chapters 19–24.) Example:

> **In the past, if a student wanted to take business classes, he or she had to wait/ and go to business school.**

1. Young people, who are interested in becoming entrepreneurs, often do not wait to put their plans into action.

2. Nowadays, even high school students are fearlessly diving in, and attempting to make a profit from their unique ideas.

3. Some teen businesspeople get under way without much guidance from adults, however, others get their start in entrepreneurship classes offered at school.

4. Such classes often provide fundamentals such as writing, speaking and accounting—but they also give students the opportunity to develop and implement their own business plans.

5. In other words, by taking these courses, teenagers get "hands-on" experience in the business world.

6. Many instructors who teach these classes receive training from the National Foundation for Teaching Entrepreneurship [NFTE].

7. According to an article in the "New York Times," founder Steve Mariotti started NFTE to help poor and minority high school students stay in school.

8. Mr Mariotti says that entrepreneurship classes empower students and teach them academic skills at the same time.

9. High school student Rodney Walker agrees that the program "sends a message that you can prosper and really do anything regardless of where you came from".

10. As an increasing number of high schools are adding entrepreneurship studies to the curriculum many colleges and universities are doing the same.

11. Fifteen or twenty years ago, very few colleges offered business courses for undergraduates, now many schools offer degree programs in the subject.

12. At a few particularly business-oriented colleges, all students are required to practice in one way or another being entrepreneurs.

13. For example, all first-year students at Babson College in Massachusetts have to start and run their own businesses!

14. Babson gives each class of twenty-five to thirty students money to put its plans into action, all profits go to charity.

15. Other schools focus on preparing their students to become *social entrepreneurs*; businesspeople who use their skills to bring about societal change.

16. Students from these universities will often go on to start nonprofit organizations, that work to eliminate poverty or to improve education.

17. Some critics argue that other more important subjects are being pushed aside, in favor of these new business classes.

18. They call entrepreneurship programs "trendy", and claim that these classes simply train students to be good capitalists.

19. Time will tell if the critic's disapproval is valid.

20. In the meantime, with or without such programs, entrepreneurial teens and college students will continue to pursue their business plans.

25.1 Capitalizing

Capitalize words as needed in the following sentences. (See *EasyWriter*, Chapter 25.) Example:

    T S E   T W   L   F   F

t. s. eliot, who wrote *the waste land*, was an editor at faber and faber.

1. the united nations campus is between first avenue and the east river in new york city.

2. the battle of lexington and concord was fought in april 1775.

3. *the lion, the witch and the wardrobe* is one of the books in the fantasy series *the chronicles of narnia* written by c. s. lewis.

4. accepting an award for his score for the film *the high and the mighty*, dmitri tiomkin thanked beethoven, brahms, wagner, and strauss.

5. i wondered if my new levi's were faded enough.

6. we drove east over the hudson river on the tappan zee bridge.

7. brazilians speak portuguese, a romance language derived from latin.

8. "bloody sunday" was a massacre of catholic protesters in derry, northern ireland, on january 30, 1972.

9. we had a choice of fast-food, chinese, or italian restaurants.

10. the town in the american south where i was raised had a statue of a civil war soldier in the center of main street.

26.1 Using abbreviations

Revise each of the following sentences to eliminate any abbreviations that would be inappropriate in academic writing. If a sentence is correct, write C. (See *EasyWriter*, 26a.) Example:

> international
> The ~~intl.~~ sport of belt sander racing began in a hardware store.
>   ^

1. Nielson Hardware in Point Roberts, WA, was the site of the world's first belt sander race in 1989.

2. The power tools, ordinarily used for sanding wood, are placed on a thirty-ft. track and plugged in; the sander to reach the end first wins.

3. Today, the International Belt Sander Drag Race Association (IBSDRA) sponsors tours of winning sanders, an international championship, and a Web site that sells IBSDRA T-shirts.

4. There are three divisions of belt sander races: the stock div., which races sanders right out of the box; the modified div., which allows any motor the owner wants to add; and the decorative div., which provides a creative outlet for sander owners.

5. An average race lasts two seconds, but the world champion modified sander raced the track in 1.52 secs.

6. The fastest sanders run on very coarse sandpaper—a no. sixteen grit is an excellent choice if it's available.

7. Stock sanders are usually widely available brands, e.g., Mikita or Bosch.

8. The S-B Power Tool Co. in Chicago, maker of Bosch sanders, allows participants to race its tools, but the co. does not underwrite races.

9. Another tool company, the Do It Best Corp. of Wayne, Ind., sponsors races across the U.S. and Canada.

10. No one knows what % of the nation's power tools have been used for this kind of entertainment.

26.2 Spelling out numbers and using figures

Revise the numbers in the following sentences as necessary for correctness and consistency. If a sentence is correct, write *C*. (See *EasyWriter*, 26b.) Example:

> *seventh*   *one*
> **No correct answer choice was given for the 7̶t̶h̶ question in part 1̶ of the test.**

1. Only one in six Afghan women ages 15-24 can read.

2. You could buy any item in the store for 99 cents.

3. The amulet measured one and one-eighth by two and two-fifths inches.

4. Walker signed a three-year, $4.5-million contract.

5. The morning of September eleven, 2001, was cool and clear in New York City.

6. Because gas was four dollars and thirty-nine cents a gallon, she decided not to go.

7. I drank 8 glasses of water, as the doctor had said, but then I had to get up 3 times during the night.

8. 307 miles long and 82 miles wide, the island offered little of interest.

9. Though seventy-five percent of people say recycling is important, only three percent recycle their old cell phones.

10. The department received 1,633 calls and forty-three letters.

27.1   Using italics

In each of the following sentences, underline any words that should be italicized, and circle any italicized words that should not be. If a title requires quotation marks instead of italicization, add them. (See *EasyWriter*, Chapter 27.) Example:

> **The United States still abounds with regional speech—for example, many people in the**
>
> **Appalachians still use local words such as <u>crick</u> and <u>holler</u>.**

1. *Regionalism*, a nineteenth-century literary movement, focused on the language and customs of people in areas of the country not yet affected by industrialization.

2. Regional writers produced some American classics, such as Mark Twain's Huckleberry Finn and James Fenimore Cooper's Last of the Mohicans.

3. Twain, not an admirer of Cooper's work, wrote a scathing essay about his predecessor called *The Literary Offenses of James Fenimore Cooper.*

4. Some of the most prolific regional writers were women such as Kate Chopin, who wrote her first collection of short stories, Bayou Folk, to help support her family.

5. The stories in *Bayou Folk*, such as the famous *Désirée's Baby*, focus on the natives of rural Louisiana.

6. Chopin also departed from regional works to explore women's experiences of marriage, as in her short piece, *The Story of an Hour.*

7. In Maine, Sarah Orne Jewett wrote sketches of rural life that appeared in the Atlantic Monthly.

8. She later turned these into a novel, Deephaven, which she hoped would "teach the world that country people were not . . . ignorant."

9. Her finest short story, *A White Heron*, and her celebrated novel *The Country of the Pointed Firs* also benefit from settings in Maine.

10. Many regional stories—Stephen Crane's *The Bride Comes to Yellow Sky* is a prime example— show the writer's concern that an isolated culture is in danger of disappearing.

28.1 Using hyphens in compounds and with prefixes

Insert hyphens as needed. A dictionary will help you with some items. If an item does not require a hyphen, write C. (See *EasyWriter*, 28a–b.) Example:

full bodied wine

1. a nineteen year old college student

2. thirty three

3. pre World War II

4. the all American soccer team

5. a hard working farmer

6. a friend who is soft spoken

7. deescalate

8. self guided

9. happily married couple

10. cutting edge technology

28.2 Using hyphens appropriately

Insert or delete hyphens as needed. Use your dictionary if necessary. If a sentence is correct as printed, write C. (See *EasyWriter,* Chapter 28.) Example:

> The bleary eyed student finally stopped fighting sleep and went to bed.

1.   The carpenter stopped to pick-up some three quarter inch nails.

2.   The name of the president elect had been announced an hour before the polls closed.

3.   We urged him to be open minded and to temper his insensitive views.

4.   Stress can lead to hypertension and ulcers.

5.   Her dolllike features fooled many observers, but her competitors soon found that she had ice-cold blood and nerves-of-steel.

6.   The ill fated antelope became the baboon's lunch.

7.   The group members worked-out their disagreements.

8.   The badly-wrapped sandwich oozed mustard and bits of soggy lettuce.

9.   Suicide among teenagers has tripled in the past thirty five years.

10. One standby passenger made the oversold flight.

•••••

30.1 Identifying stereotypes

Each of the following sentences stereotypes a person or a group of people. Underline the word or phrase that stereotypes the person or group. In each case, be ready to explain why the stereotype may be offensive, demeaning, or unfair. (See *EasyWriter*, Chapter 30.) Example:

If you have trouble printing, ask a computer geek for help.

Assumes that all computer-savvy people are geeky, which is not the case.

1. The comedy show flopped because those rednecks in the audience don't understand satire.

2. Academics are extremely well paid, considering how few hours they actually teach.

3. Their math scores are higher than ours because their school has more Asian students.

4. I would never travel to France because everyone there hates Americans.

5. College kids need real-world experience.

6. Dropouts have trouble landing good jobs.

7. When we visit the nursing home, remember to treat the old folks with respect.

8. Who knows what those Goth kids are carrying under those big trench coats?

30.2   Identifying and revising sexist language

The following excerpt is taken from the 1968 edition of Dr. Benjamin Spock's *Baby and Child Care*. Read it carefully, noting any language we might today consider sexist. Revise the passage, substituting nonsexist language as necessary. (See *EasyWriter*, 30b.)

399. Feeling his oats. One year old is an exciting age. Your baby is changing in lots of ways — in his eating, in how he gets around, in what he wants to do and in how he feels about himself and other people. When he was little and helpless, you could put him where you wanted him, give him the playthings you thought suitable, feed him the foods you knew were best. Most of the time he was willing to let you be the boss, and took it all in good spirit. It's more complicated now that he is around a year old. He seems to realize that he's not meant to be a baby doll the rest of his life, that he's a human being with ideas and a will of his own.

When you suggest something that doesn't appeal to him, he feels he must assert himself. His nature tells him to. He just says No in words or actions, even about things that he likes to do. The psychologists call it "negativism"; mothers call it "that terrible No stage." But stop and think what would happen to him if he never felt like saying No. He'd become a robot, a mechanical man. You wouldn't be able to resist the temptation to boss him all the time, and he'd stop learning and developing. When he was old enough to go out into the world, to school and later to work, everybody else would take advantage of him, too. He'd never be good for anything.

30.3 **Rewriting to eliminate offensive references**

Review the following sentences for offensive references or terms. If a sentence seems accept-able as written, write *C*. If a sentence contains unacceptable terms, rewrite it. (See *EasyWriter*, Chapter 30.) Example:

> *Passengers*
> ~~Elderly passengers~~ on the cruise ship *Romance Afloat* will enjoy swimming, shuffleboard,
> ^
> and nightly movies.

1. A West Point cadet must keep his record clean if he expects to excel in his chosen career.

2. My Oriental friend is going to teach me sign language.

3. People like mill workers probably don't listen to the classical music station.

4. Disabled state representative Greg Smith won the election yesterday.

5. If you can find a mechanic today, see if he will be able to look at the car before morning.

6. Seventy-six-year-old Jewish violinist Josh Mickle, last night's featured soloist, brought the crowd to its feet.

7. Our skylight was installed last week by a woman carpenter.

8. Please tell my male secretary that I would like to meet at three o'clock today.

9. Blind psychology professor Dr. Charles Warnath gave the keynote address last night.

10. You can call a handyman to fix the sink.

31.1 Considering ethnic and regional varieties of English

Read the following examples by authors using ethnic and regional varieties of English. See if you can "translate" each into standard academic English. Once you have your translated sentences, write a paragraph (in standard academic English) discussing (1) the differences you detect between standard academic English and the ethnic or regional example and (2) the effects that are achieved by using each variety of English. (See *EasyWriter*, Chapter 31.)

"Hey!" squeaked Curtis, his expression amazed. "I got myself shot in the back!"

Beside him, Lyon lifted Curtis' tattered T-shirt, plain and faded black like the other

boys' . . . gang colors. "Yeah? Well, you for sure be takin it cool, man. Let's check it out."

. . . Finally, he smiled and parted Curtis' arm. "It be only a cut. Like from a chunk of flyin

brick or somethin. Nowhere near his heart. That be all what matter."

—Jess Mowry, *Way Past Cool*

". . . You look like you come from here but don't sound it."

"My people came from Quoyle's Point but I was brought up in the States. So I'm an outsider. More or less." Quoyle's hand crept up over his chin.

The harbormaster looked at him. Squinted.

"Yes," said Diddy Shovel. "I guess you got a story there, m'boy. How did it all come about that you was raised so far from home? That you come back?"

—E. Annie Proulx, *The Shipping News*

32.1 **Using formal register**

Revise each of the following sentences to use formal register consistently, eliminating collo-quial or slang terms. (See *EasyWriter*, 32a.) Example:

Although be excited   as soon as   blank.
    I can ~~get all enthused~~ about writing, ~~but~~ I sit down to write my mind goes ~~right to sleep~~.

1. James Agee's most famous novel, *A Death in the Family*, focuses on a young boy and on what happens after his old man kicks in a car wreck.

2. He decided to buy his ticket while the getting was good.

3. This essay will trash Mr. Buckley's wacko argument.

4. We decided not to buy a bigger car that got lousy gas mileage and chose instead to keep our old Honda.

5. Our Spanish teacher packs a busload of information into each hour-long class.

6. After she had raced to the post office at ten minutes to five, she realized that she had completely spaced the fact that it was a federal holiday.

7. Portions of the Web are inaccessible to blind people, but creative types are coming up with new technology to help solve this problem.

8. Moby Dick's humongous size was matched only by Ahab's obsessive desire to wipe him out.

9. My family lived in Trinidad for the first ten years of my life, and we went through a lot; but when we came to America, we thought we had it made.

10. The class behaved so dreadfully in their regular teacher's absence that the substitute lost it.

32.2 **Determining levels of language**

For each of the scenarios below, note who the audience would be for the piece of writing. Then circle the level of formality that would be appropriate. Be prepared to explain your answer. (See *EasyWriter,* 32a.) Example:

> **An Internet chat room for people who are interested in Harley-Davidson motorcycles**
>
> **Level of formality:**
>
> (informal)   **formal**
>
> **Audience:** _____ *others who share your passion* _____

1. A thank-you note for a birthday gift

   Level of formality:

   informal   formal

   Audience: _____

2. An article for a magazine explaining how to get a student loan with a low interest rate

   Level of formality:

   informal   formal

   Audience: _____

3. A brochure explaining the recycling policies of your community to local residents

   Level of formality:

   informal   formal

   Audience: _____

4. A letter to the editor of the *Washington Post* explaining that a recent editorial failed to consider all the facts about health maintenance organizations (HMOs)

   Level of formality:

   informal   formal

   Audience: _____

5. A cover letter asking a professor to accept the late paper you are sending after the end of the semester.

   Level of formality:

   informal   formal

   Audience: _____

32.3 Checking for correct denotation

Read each of the following sentences, looking for errors in denotation. Use your dictionary as needed. Underline every error that you find, determine the word intended, and write in the correct word. If a sentence has no error, write C. (See *EasyWriter*, 32b.) Example:

species
The polar bear ~~spaces~~ is threatened by the loss of habitat due to climate change.

1. Polar bears live on the icy coasts of antarctic North America.

2. The largest land carnival in the Arctic, the polar bear is at the top of the arctic marine food chain.

3. Biologists esteem that there are at least 22,000 polar bears in the wild and that about 60 percent live in Canada.

4. People who have only seen polar bears in zoos probably don't realize how detached they are to their environment.

5. Polar bears depend on sea ice for hunting and forging.

6. Seals are polar bears' primary pray, but the bears also hunt walrus, beluga whales, fish, and sea birds.

7. Polar bears hunt seals by waiting silently at a seal's breathing hole in the ice and bouncing on the seal when it comes up for air.

8. The main threat to polar bears today is the loss of sea ice due to global warming.

9. Though the Arctic has experienced warm periods in the past, the current melting of sea ice has no president.

10. While an argument signed by Canada, the United States, Denmark, Norway, and the former Soviet Union in 1973 restricts the hunting of polar bears, it does not protect the bears from global warming.

32.4 Revising sentences to change connotation

The sentences that follow contain words with strongly judgmental connotative meanings. Underline these words; then revise each sentence to make it more neutral. (See *EasyWriter*, 32b.) Example:

> The current NRA <u>scheme</u> appeals to patriotism as a <u>smoke screen to obscure the real issue</u>
>
> <u>of gun control.</u>
>
> The current NRA campaign appeals to patriotism rather than responding directly to gun-control proposals.

1. The Democrats are conspiring on a new education bill.

2. CEOs waltz away with millions in salary, stock options, and pensions, whereas the little people who keep the company running get peanuts.

3. Religious freaks staged protests on the campaign trail.

4. Tree-huggers ranted about the Explorer's gas mileage outside the Ford dealership.

5. The bookworm managed to grub another A in history.

6. The Internet is riddled with sites peddling hogwash.

7. Liberals constantly whine about protecting civil rights, but they don't care about protecting the flag that Americans have fought and died for.

8. A mob of protesters appeared, yelling and jabbing their signs in the air.

32.5 Considering connotation

Study the italicized words in each of the following passages, and decide what each word's connotations contribute to your understanding of the passage. Think of a synonym for each word. What difference would the new word make to the effect of the passage? (See *EasyWriter*, 32b.) Example:

> It is a story of extended horror. But it isn't only the horror that *numbs* response. Nor is it that the discoverer [Columbus] *deteriorates* so steadily after the discovery. It is the *banality* of the man. He was looking less for America or Asia than for gold; and the banality of expectation matches a continuing banality of *perception*.
>
> —V. S. Naipaul, "Columbus and Crusoe"

numbs: deadens, paralyzes
deteriorates: declines, gets worse
banality: ordinariness, triviality
perception: understanding, judgment

1. The Burmans were already *racing* past me across the mud. It was obvious that the elephant would never *rise* again, but he was not dead. He was breathing very rhythmically with long *rattling* gasps, his great *mound* of a side painfully rising and falling.

    —George Orwell, "Shooting an Elephant"

2. Then one evening Miss Glory told me to serve the ladies on the porch. After I set the tray down and turned toward the kitchen, one of the women asked, "What's your name, *girl*?"

    —Maya Angelou, *I Know Why the Caged Bird Sings*

3. We caught two bass, *hauling* them in *briskly* as though they were mackerel, pulling them over the side of the boat in a *businesslike* manner without any landing net, and stunning them with a *blow* on the back of the head.

    —E. B. White, "Once More to the Lake"

4. The Kiowas are a summer people; they *abide* the cold and keep to themselves; but when the season *turns* and the land becomes warm and *vital*, they cannot *hold still*.

    —N. Scott Momaday, "The Way to Rainy Mountain"

5. If boxing is a sport, it is the most *tragic* of all sports because, more than any [other] human activity, it *consumes* the very excellence it *displays*: Its very *drama* is this consumption.

    —Joyce Carol Oates, "On Boxing"

32.6   Using specific and concrete words

Rewrite each of the following sentences to be more specific and more concrete. (See *EasyWriter*, 32c.) Example:

> **The weather this summer has varied.**
>
> *July and August have offered two extremes of weather, going from clear, dry days, on which the breeze seems to scrub the sky, to the dog days of oppressive humidity.*

1. They live in the house down the street.

2. The museum is filled with great artwork.

3. The camp is on a few acres by the lake.

4. Children sometimes behave badly in public.

5. The entryway of the building was dirty.

6. Robert was not feeling well, so he stayed home from the party.

7. My neighbor is a nuisance.

8. Sunday dinner was good.

9. The sounds at dawn are memorable.

10. Central Texas has an unusual climate.

32.7 **Thinking about similes and metaphors**

Identify the similes and metaphors in the following numbered items, and decide how each contributes to your understanding of the passage or sentence in which it appears. (See *Easy-Writer*, 32d.) Example:

> **The tattoo he had gotten as a teenager, now a blue bruise underneath the word "Mom,"**
>
> **remained his favorite souvenir.**
>
> *a blue bruise* (metaphor): makes vivid the tattoo's appearance

1. The fog hangs among the trees like veils of trailing lace.
   –Stephanie Vaughn, "My Mother Breathing Light"

2. The clouds were great mounds of marshmallow fluff heaped just below the wings of the passing airplane.

3. The migraine acted as a circuit breaker, and the fuses have emerged intact.
   –Joan Didion, "In Bed"

4. As Serena began to cry, James felt as if someone had punched him in the stomach.

5. Black women are called, in the folklore that so aptly identifies one's status in society, "the mule of the world," because we have been handed the burdens that everyone else—everyone else—refused to carry.
   –Alice Walker, *In Search of Our Mothers' Gardens*

6. John's mother, Mom Willie, who wore her Southern background like a magnolia corsage, eternally fresh, was robust and in her sixties.
   –Maya Angelou, "The Heart of a Woman"

7. According to Dr. Seuss, the Grinch is a bad banana with a greasy black peel.

8. I was watching everyone else and didn't see the waitress standing quietly by. Her voice was deep and soft like water moving in a cavern.
   –William Least Heat Moon, "In the Land of 'Coke-Cola'"

9. The clicking sounds of the rotary phone were as old-fashioned and charming as the song of a square dance caller.

10. My horse, when he is in his stall or lounging about the pasture, has the same relationship to pain that I have when cuddling up with a good murder mystery—comfort and convenience have top priority.
    –Vicki Hearne, "Horses in Partnership with Time"

• • • • •

34.1 Expressing subjects and objects explicitly

Revise the following sentences or nonsentences as necessary so that they have explicit subjects and objects. If a sentence does not contain an error, write C. (See *EasyWriter,* 34a.) Example:

It is
~~Is~~ easy and convenient for people with access to computers to shop online.
  ^

1. No faster way to take care of holiday shopping.

2. Computers also allow people to buy items they cannot find locally.

3. Banks and credit-card companies have Web sites now, and consumers use for making payments, looking at statements, and transferring balances.

4. Are problems with doing everything online, of course.

5. Customers must use credit cards, and thieves want to break in and get.

6. Are small-time thieves and pranksters disrupting online services.

7. Jamming popular sites is one way for hackers to gain notoriety, and have been several examples of this action.

8. A hacker can get enormous amounts of online data, even if is supposed to be secure.

9. People should be concerned about online privacy because is a tremendous amount of private information stored in online databases.

10. Internet users must use caution and common sense online, but is also essential for online information to be safeguarded by security experts.

34.2 **Editing for English word order**

Revise the following sentences as necessary. If a sentence does not contain an error, write C. (See *EasyWriter,* 34b.) Example:

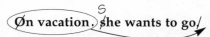

1. To sleep he wishes to go now.

2. He displays proudly in the window a flag.

3. Comes in first the runner from Kenya.

4. She should go not into the woods alone.

5. A passing grade she wants.

6. Promptly the train arrives at six o'clock.

7. The class laughed frequently throughout the lecture.

8. Friends I like to go to the movies with.

9. John watches videos incessantly.

10. "Spend carefully your money," advised my mother.

35.1 Identifying count and noncount nouns

Identify each of the common nouns in the following paragraph as either a count or a non-count noun. (See *EasyWriter*, 35a.) The first one has been done for you.

> *count*
> In his book *Hiroshima*, John Hersey tells the story of six people who survived the destruction of Hiroshima on August 6, 1945. The bomb detonated at 8:15 in the morning. When the explosion occurred, Mrs. Hatsuyo Nakamura was looking out her window and watching a neighbor at work on his house. The force of the explosion lifted her into the air and carried her into the next room, where she was buried by roofing tiles and other debris. When she crawled out, she heard her daughter, Myeko, calling out; she was buried up to her waist and could not move.

35.2 Using appropriate noun phrases

Each of the following sentences contains at least one error with a noun phrase. Revise each sentence. (See *EasyWriter*, 35b.) Example:

                                    a
    Many people use small sponge to clean their kitchen counters.
                       ^

1. Bacteria are invisible organisms that can sometimes make the people sick.

2. Dangerous germs, such as salmonella, are commonly found in a some foods.

3. When a cook prepares chicken on cutting board, salmonella germs may be left on the board.

4. Much people regularly clean their kitchen counters and cutting boards to remove bacteria.

5. Unfortunately, a warm, wet kitchen sponge is a ideal home for bacteria.

6. Every time someone wipes a counter with dirty sponge, more germ are spread around the kitchen.

7. Microwaving a dirty sponge for one minute will kill a most bacteria that live in it.

8. According to research studies, the young single men's kitchens tend to have a fewer germs than other kitchen.

9. These surprising fact tells researchers that young single men do not often wipe their kitchen counters.

35.3 **Using articles appropriately**

Insert articles as necessary in the following passage. If no article is needed, leave the space blank. (See *EasyWriter*, 35c.) Example:

One of _the_ **things that makes** _____ **English unique is** _the_ **number of** _____ **English words.**

_____ English language has _____ very large vocabulary. About _____ 200,000 words are in _____ everyday use, and if _____ less common words are included, _____ total reaches more than _____ million. This makes _____ English _____ rich language, but also _____ difficult one to learn well. In addition, _____ rules of English grammar are sometimes confusing. They were modeled on _____ Latin rules, even though _____ two languages are very different. Finally, _____ fact that _____ English has _____ large number of _____ words imported from _____ other languages makes _____ English spelling very hard to master. _____ English is now _____ most widely used language around _____ world, so _____ educated people are expected to know it.

36.1 **Identifying verbs and verb phrases**

Underline each verb or verb phrase in the following sentences. (See *Easy Writer,* Chapter 36.)
Example:

Many cultures <u>celebrate</u> the arrival of spring with a festival of some kind.

1. The spring festival of Holi occurs in northern India every March during the full moon.

2. Holi is known as the festival of colors, not only because spring brings flowers, but also because Holi celebrations always include brightly colored dyes.

3. According to legend, the festival of colors began thousands of years ago when Krishna played pranks on girls in his village and threw water on them.

4. During Holi, people toss fistfuls of powdered dyes or dye-filled water balloons at each other and sing traditional Holi songs.

5. Holi festivals allow people freedoms that would be unthinkable during the rest of the year.

6. Any person who is walking outside during a Holi celebration will soon be wearing colored powders or colored water.

7. Men, women, and children can throw powders or dye-filled balloons at anyone, even if the person is much older or of much higher status than they are.

8. Many people wear white clothing for Holi.

9. By the end of the celebration, the white clothes are a riot of color.

10. Doesn't Holi sound like fun?

36.2 Using the present, present perfect, and past forms of verbs

Rewrite the following passage by adding appropriate forms of *have* and main-verb endings or forms for the verbs in parentheses. (See *EasyWriter*, 36a.) Example:

I _____like_____ **(like) to try new foods, so I** __have eaten__ **(eat) in many different kinds of restaurants in my life.**

Several times, I _____ (hear) people musing about the bravery of the first person who ever _____ (eat) a lobster. It _____ (be) an interesting question: what do you _____ (think) _____ (make) anyone do such a thing? But personally, I _____ (wonder) all my life about how ancient people _____ (discover) the art of baking bread. After all, preparing a lobster _____ (be) pretty simple in comparison to baking. Bread _____ (feed) vast numbers of people for centuries, so it certainly _____ (be) a more important food source than lobster, too. Those of us who _____ (love) either lobster or bread (or both) _____ (be) grateful to those who _____ (give) us such a wonderful culinary legacy.

36.3 Using specified forms of verbs

Using the subjects and verbs provided, write the specified sentences. (See *EasyWriter*, 36a.)
Example:

> **subject:** *Bernie*   **verb:** *touch*
>
> **sentence using a present form:** Bernie touches the soft fur.
>
> **sentence using the auxiliary verb *had*:** Bernie had touched a squid before.

1. subject: *they*   verb: *decide*

   sentence using a present form:

   sentence using an auxiliary verb + the past participle form:

2. subject: *someone*   verb: *follow*

   sentence using a past form:

   sentence using an auxiliary verb + the present participle form:

3. subject: *we*   verb: *ask*

   sentence using a present form:

   sentence using the auxiliary *had* + the past participle form:

4. subject: *geese*   verb: *migrate*

   sentence using a past form:

   sentence using an auxiliary verb + the present participle form:

5. subject: *student*   verb: *volunteer*

   sentence using a present form:

   sentence using an auxiliary verb + a past participle form:

6. subject: *teenagers*   verb: *consume*

   sentence using a past form:

   sentence using the auxiliary verb *were* + the present participle form:

7. subject: *judge*   verb: *expect*

   sentence using a present form:

   sentence using an auxiliary verb + a present participle form:

8. subject: *father*   verb: *cook*

   sentence using a present form:

   sentence using an auxiliary verb + a present participle form:

9. subject: *pilots*   verb: *fly*

   sentence using a past form:

   sentence using an auxiliary verb + a present participle form:

10. subject: *artists*   verb: *work*

    sentence using a present form:

    sentence using an auxiliary verb + a past participle form:

36.4 Identifying tenses and forms of verbs

From the following list, identify the form of each verb or verb phrase in each of the numbered sentences. (See *EasyWriter*, 36a.)

simple present	past perfect
simple past	present progressive
present perfect	past progressive

Example:

> **Judge Cohen considered the two arguments.**   *Simple past*

1. On the right side of the room, Monica is demonstrating the Heimlich maneuver.

2. The tennis champion had beaten her opponent in the last tournament.

3. Brian is applying for a Fulbright Scholarship.

4. I have asked for directions three times today.

5. Just as we took our seats, the movie began.

6. Eden danced with the city ballet company for seven years.

7. Paul required special medical attention for years.

8. My mother has driven the same Mazda for ten years.

9. Horror movies rarely make much of an impression on me, but this one has made me afraid to go out into the parking lot.

10. She had forgotten the assignment.

36.5 Using verbs appropriately

Each of the following sentences contains an error with verbs. Revise each sentence. (See *Easy-Writer*, 36a.) Example:

             could not
    Linguists ~~cannot~~ interpret hieroglyphics before they discovered the Rosetta Stone.

1. A French engineer was finding a stone half-buried in the mud by the Nile River in Egypt in 1799.

2. The Rosetta Stone is cover with inscriptions in three ancient languages.

3. The inscription at the top of the stone written in Egyptian hieroglyphics, or pictographs, while the lower part gives the same information in an ancient Egyptian language called Demotic and in ancient Greek.

4. At that time, scholars were puzzled by hieroglyphics for centuries.

5. Very soon after its discovery, the French have made copies of the stone.

6. A scholar named Jean François Champollion could understood both ancient Greek and modern Egyptian, known as Coptic.

7. Champollion knew that he can figure out the Demotic script based on his knowledge of Coptic.

8. From the Demotic inscription, he has learned to read the hieroglyphics.

9. The story of the Rosetta Stone is probably more fascinated than the contents of its inscription.

10. The hieroglyphics and the Demotic and Greek texts all are containing a decree from an ancient king.

36.6 Using infinitives and gerunds appropriately

Revise the following sentences as necessary so that each contains an appropriate infinitive or gerund positioned well. If a sentence does not contain an error, write C. (See *EasyWriter*, 36a–b.) Example:

> that
> It pleases me ᴧyou like me.

1. We discussed to go to a movie, but we could not agree on what to see.

2. Ashok refused answering his sister's questions.

3. Her mother stopped to drive on her ninetieth birthday.

4. What he has to say is of great interest to me.

5. No one expected being allowed to leave work before midnight.

6. We appreciated to get the invitation.

37.2 Recognizing and using two-word verbs

Identify each italicized expression as either a two-word verb or a verb + preposition. (See *EasyWriter*, 37b.) Example:

> ***Look up*** **John Brown the next time you're in town.**   *two-word verb*

1. George was still *looking for* his keys when we left.

2. I always *turn down* the thermostat when I go to bed or leave the house.

3. We drank a pitcher of lemonade in an attempt to *cool* ourselves *off* on a sweltering July afternoon.

4. Marion *gave back* the ring she had gotten as an engagement gift.

5. Jimmy *takes after* his father, poor thing.

6. The car *turned into* the driveway.

7. The frog *turned into* a prince.

8. The camp counselor *handed* the candy *out* as if it were gold.

9. *Put* the garbage *out* on the sidewalk, please.

10. Don't *put* yourself *out* on my behalf.

Answers to the Even-Numbered Exercises

FIND IT. FIX IT.

Recognizing and eliminating the twenty most common errors

2. [Poorly integrated quotation] According to Jane Austen's *Pride and Prejudice*, "It is a truth universally acknowledged, that a single man in possession of a good fortune must be in want of a wife" (1).

4. [Wrong word] The three students from African countries in our international studies class bring a valuable perspective to discussions about politics in developing nations.

6. [Missing comma in a compound sentence] Kevin enjoys watching auto racing and golf, but his brother prefers to watch baseball.

8. [Spelling (including homonyms)] I couldn't believe it when I noticed Todd driving with bare feet!

10. [Unnecessary or missing capitalization] The Galapagos Islands are an archipelago of volcanic islands west of South America.

12. [Missing comma with a nonrestrictive element] The Beastie Boys, who have been together since 1979, tour frequently.

14. [Unnecessary shift in verb tense] The coxswain quickly barked orders to the rowers on his team, and the crowd cheered wildly.

16. [Unnecessary or missing apostrophe (including *its/it's*)] The great white shark is a carnivorous animal known for its large jaw and sharp teeth.

18. [Mechanical error with a quotation] Edgar Allan Poe's dark short story "The Cask of Amontillado" begins, "The thousand injuries of Fortunato I had borne as best I could; but when he ventured upon insult, I vowed revenge."

20. [Missing word] Uncle George asked me to turn on the gas and let the barbecue warm up.

WRITING

EXERCISE 3.2   Recognizing arguable statements

2. factual

4. factual

6. arguable

8. factual

10. arguable

SENTENCE GRAMMAR

EXERCISE 7.1   Identifying verbs

2. climbed; was

4. drop; is

6. was; froze

8. warmed

10. is

EXERCISE 7.2   Using irregular verb forms

2. was; said; was

4. broke; lay

6. met; fell

8. kept; was

10. grown; spread

EXERCISE 7.3   Editing verb forms

2. had gave—given

4. ate—eaten

6. C

8. knowed—known

10. C

EXERCISE 7.4   Distinguishing between *lie* and *lay*, *sit* and *set*, *rise* and *raise*

2. lying

4. rose

6. set

8. set

10. lies

EXERCISE 7.5   Deciding on verb tenses

2. celebrated

4. know; took

6. lit; made; wore

8. resembles

10. aim

EXERCISE 7.6   Sequencing tenses

2. Until I saw the sequel, I *had expected* a tragic ending.

4. After Darius said that he wanted to postpone college, I *tried* to talk him out of it.

6. The senator *had hoped* to be ahead in the polls by now.

8. C

10. *Having cut off* all contact with family, he had no one to ask for help.

EXERCISE 7.7   Converting the voice of a sentence

Answers may vary slightly.

2. Airline officials *recovered* the black boxes.

4. Jerry *ate* the last doughnut in the box just a few minutes ago.

6. For months, the mother kangaroo *protects*, *feeds*, and *teaches* its baby how to survive.

8. The first snow of winter *covered* the lawns and rooftops.

10. Suddenly, the roof over our heads *was being pounded on* by rainfall.

EXERCISE 7.8   Using the subjunctive mood

2. is—be

4. would have—had

6. knows—know

8. should not take—not take

10. would have—had

EXERCISE 8.1   Selecting verbs that agree with their subjects

2. are

4. include

6. offer

8. looks

10. does

EXERCISE 8.2   Making subjects and verbs agree

2. are—is

4. use—uses

6. sets—set

8. C

10. allows—allow

12. C

14. belongs—belong

EXERCISE 9.1   Identifying adjectives and adverbs

Adjectives are set in *italics;* adverbs are set in **boldface**.

2. *small;* **noisily;** *the; the; front*

4. *The; dilapidated; tour;* **steadily;** *the; winding; the; steep*

6. *The; youngest; the; a; brilliant*

8. *The;* **eagerly;** *the; delicious; the*

10. *The; history;* **excitedly;** *the; fascinating; the*

EXERCISE 9.2   Adding adjectives and adverbs

SUGGESTED ANSWERS

2. Surely, most of us enjoy classic movies.

4. The stern judge addresses the silent jury.

6. A visitor can sometimes learn the native language quickly.

8. The mainstream media are determinedly ignoring his candidacy.

10. Why did the man run frantically back to the burning house?

EXERCISE 9.3   Using adjectives and adverbs appropriately

2. defiant—defiantly; modifies *crosses*

4. sadly—sad; modifies *you*

6. relievedly—relieved; modifies *you*

8. oddly—odd; modifies *"words"*

10. Lucky—Luckily; modifies *available*

EXERCISE 9.4   Using comparative and superlative modifiers appropriately

SUGGESTED ANSWERS

2. to live longer—to live longer than men

4. largest—larger

6. famousest—most famous

8. unpleasantest—most unpleasant

10. the most unique—a unique

EXERCISE 10.1   Revising sentences with misplaced modifiers

SUGGESTED ANSWERS

2. The tenor, singing with verve, captivated the entire audience.

4. The city spent approximately twelve million dollars on the new stadium.

6. On the day in question, the patient was not able to breathe normally.

8. The clothes that I was giving away were full of holes.

10. A wailing baby with a soggy diaper was quickly kissed by the candidate.

EXERCISE 10.2   Revising squinting modifiers, disruptive modifiers, and split infinitives

SUGGESTED ANSWERS

2. He vividly remembered enjoying the sound of Mrs. McIntosh's singing.

4. The mayor promised that she would not raise taxes after her reelection.
    After her reelection, the mayor promised that she would not raise taxes.

6. The hardware store where we recently bought lightbulbs went out of business.
    The hardware store where we bought lightbulbs went out of business recently.

8. Doctors can now restore limbs that have been partially severed to a functioning condition.
    Doctors can now restore limbs that have been severed to a partially functioning condition.

10. The speaker said he would answer questions when he finished.
    When he finished, the speaker said he would answer questions.

12. After a day of rain, the temperature dropped, causing black ice to form on the roads.

14. After a long day at work and an evening class, Stella did not want to argue about who was going to do the dishes.
    Stella did not want to argue about who was going to do the dishes after a long day at work and an evening class.

EXERCISE 10.3   Revising dangling modifiers

SUGGESTED ANSWERS

2. A video that spreads to a large audience over a short period of time is often compared to a virus.

4. Usually short and often funny, these videos generally exist for entertainment.

6. Using simple equipment and editing techniques, amateurs can turn home movies into viral videos.

8. Clips of funny moments from TV shows are posted on video-sharing sites.

10. Videos that highlight famous people's mistakes, missteps, or other private matters are sometimes embarrassing.

12. Hoping to become famous even for doing something stupid, some attention-seeking people post videos.

14. Thriving on publicity, politicians, advertisers, and activists have also sought viral video fame.

EXERCISE 11.1   Identifying pronouns and antecedents

Pronouns are set in *italics*; antecedents are set in **boldface**.

2. **dogs**; *that*; *their*

4. *they*; *their*; **volunteers**; **puppy**; *its*

6. *you*; **puppy**; *its*; **coat**; *that*; *it*

8. *Some*; **pups**; *these*

10. *you*; *your*

EXERCISE 11.2   Using subjective-case pronouns

2. they

4. they

6. they

8. We

10. she

EXERCISE 11.3   Using objective-case pronouns

2. C

4. When we asked, the seller promised us that the software would work on a Macintosh computer.

6. Max told Jackson and him that the cabin was available to them.

8. C

10. We need two volunteers: you and Tom.

EXERCISE 11.4   Using possessive-case pronouns

2. mine

4. Her

6. their

8. her

10. yours

EXERCISE 11.5   Using *who, whoever, whom,* or *whomever*

2. Whoever

4. whomever

6. Whom

8. whom

10. whoever

EXERCISE 11.6   Using pronouns in compound structures, appositives, elliptical clauses; choosing between *we* and *us* before a noun

2. We

4. he

6. her

8. them

10. she

12. us

14. I

EXERCISE 11.7   Maintaining pronoun-antecedent agreement

SUGGESTED ANSWERS

2. A child-free person may feel that people with children see his or her time as less valuable than their own.

4. Child-free employees may feel that they have to subsidize family medical plans at work for people who have children.

6. However, a community has to consider the welfare of its children because caring for and educating children eventually benefits everyone.

8. Almost no one would be able to afford to have children if parents were expected to pay for educating and training their offspring entirely without help.

10. As writer Barbara Kingsolver once pointed out, even people without children will probably need the services of a doctor or a mechanic in their old age.

EXERCISE 11.8   Clarifying pronoun reference

SUGGESTED ANSWERS

2. Not long after the company set up the subsidiary, the subsidiary went bankrupt.

    Not long after the company set up the subsidiary, the company went bankrupt.

4. When Deyon was reunited with his father, the boy wept.

    When Deyon was reunited with his father, his father wept.

6. The weather forecast said to expect snow in the overnight hours.

8. Lear divides his kingdom between the two older daughters, Goneril and Regan, whose extravagant professions of love are more flattering than the simple affection of the youngest daughter, Cordelia. The consequences of this error in judgment soon become apparent, as the older daughters prove neither grateful nor kind to him.

10. The visit to the pyramids was canceled because of recent terrorist attacks on tourists there, so Kay, who had waited years to see the monuments, was disappointed.

EXERCISE 12.1   Revising comma splices and fused sentences

Only one suggested answer is given for each numbered item.

2. The group Human Rights Watch filed a report on Mauritania, a nation in northwest Africa.

4. Members of Mauritania's ruling group are called the Beydanes, an Arab Berber tribe also known as the White Moors.

6. In modern-day Mauritania, many of the Haratin are still slaves; they serve the Beydanes.

8. Mauritania outlawed slavery in 1981, but little has been done to enforce the law.

10. Physical force is not usually used to enslave the Haratin. Rather, they are held by the force of conditioning.

12. By some estimates 300,000 former slaves, who are psychologically and economically dependent, still serve their old masters.

14. In addition, there may be as many as 90,000 Haratin still enslaved; some Beydanes have refused to free their slaves unless the government pays compensation.

16. Of course, slavery must have existed in Mauritania, or there would have been no compelling reason to make a decree to abolish it in 1981.

18. Both the slaveholding Beydanes and the enslaved Haratin are made up largely of Muslims, so some people in Mauritania see resistance to slavery in their country as anti-Muslim.

20. Islamic authorities in Mauritania have agreed that all Muslims are equal; therefore, one Muslim must not enslave another.

EXERCISE 13.1   Eliminating sentence fragments

SUGGESTED ANSWERS

2. Her father pulled strings to get her the job. Later he regretted his actions.

4. I must have looked ridiculous trying to carry a portfolio, art box, illustration boards, and drawing pads.

6. Stephenie Meyer wrote her young adult novel *Twilight* after the idea for the book came to her in a dream. She later produced three sequels.

8. The region has dry, sandy soil, blown into strange formations by the ever-present wind.

10. Many immigrants come to the United States to find jobs that can support their families.

SENTENCE STYLE

EXERCISE 14.1   Matching subjects and predicates

SUGGESTED ANSWERS

2. Many of her books deal with the aftermath of slavery and often feature strong women characters.
    Her books, many of which deal with the aftermath of slavery, often feature strong women characters.

4. Although Morrison's depictions of African American families and neighborhoods are realistic, they also include supernatural elements.

   Morrison's depictions of African American families and neighborhoods are realistic, but they also include supernatural elements.

6. *Song of Solomon* was hailed as a masterpiece, winning the National Book Critics Circle Award in 1978.

   Song of Solomon, hailed as a masterpiece, won the National Book Critics Circle Award in 1978.

8. The title character in *Beloved* is the ghost of a murdered infant inhabiting the body of a young woman.

   Beloved features the ghost of a murdered infant inhabiting the body of a young woman.

10. In 1993, Toni Morrison became the first African American woman to be awarded the Nobel Prize in literature.

    Toni Morrison, who was awarded the Nobel Prize in literature in 1993, was the first African American woman to win that prize.

EXERCISE 14.2 Making comparisons complete, consistent, and clear

SUGGESTED ANSWERS

2. Mr. Jones's motorcycle is older than Mr. Murray's convertible and John's car.

4. During spring break, Vanessa decided to visit her family in Canada, Roger decided to travel to Costa Rica, and James decided to return to his hometown.

6. The car's exterior is blue, but the seats are black vinyl.

8. Are colleges in the United States as competitive as or more competitive than they were five years ago?

10. She argued that children are even more important for men than they are for women.

EXERCISE 15.1 Identifying conjunctions

2. and; while

4. When

6. and; until

EXERCISE 15.3 Writing sentences with subordination

SUGGESTED ANSWERS

2. At my parents' house, I spent a long night on a sleep sofa that has an uncomfortably thin mattress with a hard metal bar beneath it.

4. Walking into the shelter, I saw men, women, and children slumped against the wall, their belongings lying in overturned shopping carts.

EXERCISE 16.1　Eliminating unnecessary words and phrases

SUGGESTED ANSWERS

2. Shortly after Houdini's birth, his family moved to Appleton, where his father served as the only rabbi.

4. His many escapes included getting out of a giant sealed envelope without tearing it and walking out of jail cells that were said to be escape-proof.

6. Clearly, Houdini did not want anyone to know his secrets.

8. Houdini's tremendous control over almost every muscle allowed him to contort his body into seemingly impossible positions.

10. On his deathbed, Houdini promised his wife that he would try to make contact with her from beyond the grave, but so far, he has not been able to get in touch.

EXERCISE 17.1　Creating parallel words or phrases

SUGGESTED ANSWERS

2. I want not only hot fudge but also whipped cream.

4. I told my younger sister to keep out of my clothes and to keep away from my friends.

6. When he got his promotion, he told the neighbors, called his family, and took out an ad in the newspaper.

8. We must either walk quickly or drive slowly.

10. A good leader must guide and inspire.

EXERCISE 17.2　Revising sentences for parallelism

SUGGESTED ANSWERS

2. Many people in this country remember dancing to the mambo music of the 1950s and listening to that era's Latin bands.

4. Growing up near Havana and studying classical piano, Pérez Prado loved Cuban music.

6. Playing piano in Havana nightclubs, arranging music for a Latin big band, and joining jam sessions with the band's guitarists gave him the idea for a new kind of music.

8. Prado conducted his orchestra by waving his hands, moving his head and shoulders, and kicking his feet high in the air.

10. Pérez Prado, an innovator and a great musician, died in 1989.

EXERCISE 18.1　Revising for verb tense and mood

SUGGESTED ANSWERS

2. Today, many people still go into nature when they need to do some soul-searching.

4. Studies continue to show that being in a natural setting helps reduce people's stress levels.

6. Take your children to the park frequently, and see the difference for yourself.

8. In this study, the children who took walks in green spaces showed an improved ability to concentrate.

10. C

EXERCISE 18.2 Eliminating shifts in voice and point of view

SUGGESTED ANSWERS

2. The painters covered the furniture with drop cloths and protected the floors with plastic sheets.

4. When someone says "roommate" to a high school senior bound for college, that senior conjures up thoughts of no privacy and potential fights.

6. We knew that we shouldn't walk across the railroad trestle, but we went ahead anyway.

8. Lionel gathered the roses and then arranged them.

10. Suddenly we heard an explosion of wings off to our right, and we could see a hundred or more ducks lifting off from the water.

EXERCISE 18.3 Eliminating shifts between direct and indirect discourse

SUGGESTED ANSWERS

2. She said that during a semester abroad she really missed all her friends.

4. Loren Eiseley feels an urge to join the birds in their soundless flight, but in the end he understands that he cannot because he is "only a man."

EXERCISE 18.4 Eliminating shifts in tone and diction

SUGGESTED ANSWERS

2. The Chinese invented noodles, though many people believe the Italians created them.

4. Many activists try to publicize their cause by talking to pedestrians.

PUNCTUATION/MECHANICS

EXERCISE 19.1 Using a comma to set off introductory elements

2. In the past,

4. Of course,

6. Someday,

8. Naturally,

10. Unable to judge whether smells are delectable or nauseating,

EXERCISE 19.2 Using a comma in compound sentences

Suggested answers

2. Over two decades ago, fertility treatments were a little-explored field, so the first "test-tube baby" astonished the world.

4. A scientist combines an egg cell and a sperm cell, and an embryo forms when the egg cell begins to divide.

6. The procedure requires scientific intervention, yet the parents of a "test-tube baby" have a child that is biologically theirs.

8. In vitro fertilization has helped many people have children, but it is expensive.

10. The first "test-tube baby," who was born in England, was a celebrity, but today, children whose parents used in vitro fertilization are quite common.

EXERCISE 19.3 Recognizing restrictive and nonrestrictive elements

2. The clause *who suffers from asthma* is essential to the sentence's meaning. Therefore, it should not take commas.

4. The clause *Death of a Salesman* is essential to the sentence's meaning, so it should not take commas.

6. The appositive phrase *the first African American to serve on the U.S. Supreme Court* provides nonessential information. Therefore, the phrase requires commas to set it off.

8. The appositive phrase *the founders of Apple Computer* is nonrestrictive because it provides additional, not essential, information. Therefore, it should be set off with commas.

10. The clause *which had spared Waterville* is nonrestrictive because it provides additional, not essential, information. Therefore, it should be set off with commas.

EXERCISE 19.4 Using commas to set off items in a series

2. I am looking forward to turning eighteen, being able to vote, and perhaps serving in the military.

4. The moon circles the earth, the earth revolves around the sun, and the sun is just one star among many in the Milky Way galaxy.

6. C

8. The firm's quiet, pleasant, excessively polite public relations executives made everyone a little nervous.

10. The orientation packet for visiting students outlined the essentials: what to bring, what to expect, where to go on the first day.

EXERCISE 19.5 Using commas to set off parenthetical and transitional expressions, contrasting elements, interjections, direct address, and tag questions

2. However, we believe that democracy is the most effective form of government.

4. You've studied the formulas for the math test, haven't you?

6. Captain Kirk, I'm a doctor, not a madman.

8. One must consider the society as a whole, not just its parts.

10. Mary announced, "Kids, I want you to clean your rooms, not make a bigger mess."

EXERCISE 19.6   Using commas with dates, addresses, and quotations

2. C

4. "Who can match the desperate humorlessness of the adolescent who thinks he is the first to discover seriousness?" asks P. J. Kavanaugh.

6. The ship was hit by two torpedoes on May 7, 1915, and sank in minutes.

EXERCISE 19.7   Eliminating unnecessary and inappropriate commas

2. Insomniacs do indeed wake up at night, but studies have demonstrated that they also have trouble napping during the day.

4. In many cases, insomniacs suffer from anxiety.

6. C

8. Sleep therapists recommend going to bed at the same time every night, not watching television in bed, and not reading in bed.

10. Although tired people are more dangerous drivers and less productive workers, no one knows for certain if insomnia can actually make them sick.

EXERCISE 20.1   Using semicolons to link clauses

2. Pilates exercise includes specific strength and balance exercises combined with focused breathing patterns; as a result, people experience increased lung capacity, better circulation, and improved strength, flexibility, and balance.

4. The unwanted package arrived C.O.D.; I politely refused to pay the charges.

6. Pittsburgh was once notorious for its smoke and grime; today, its skies and streets are cleaner than those of many other American cities.

8. Establishing your position in an office is an important task; your profile will mold your relationships with other staff members.

10. Florida's mild winter climate is ideal for bicycling; in addition, the terrain is very flat.

EXERCISE 20.2   Eliminating misused semicolons

2. Mei Ching was born in the Year of the Horse, while her sister was born in the Year of the Rooster.

4. Finally, I found her at the Humane Society: a beautiful shepherd-collie mix who likes children and plays well with cats.

6. He left a large estate, which was used to endow a scholarship fund.

8. Working full-time and going to school is not always possible despite what some people may tell you.

10. The speech made sense to some observers, but not to me.

EXERCISE 21.1 Using periods appropriately

2. The appointment of Ban Ki-moon to a powerful leadership position surprised some people.

4. Though he does not have a PhD, he has decades of experience in international relations and knows five languages.

6. He has a reputation for being a hard worker who does not think twice about starting his work-day at 5:00 a.m.

8. Mr. Ban stresses the importance of this issue in his conversations with world leaders.

10. Preserving human rights and working for peace worldwide are also part of the job.

EXERCISE 21.2 Using question marks appropriately

2. "Is this the best route to the museum?" Olivia asked the cab driver.

4. "How long are we supposed to wait for Sara?" wondered Erin.

6. C

8. C

EXERCISE 21.3 Using exclamation points appropriately

SUGGESTED ANSWERS

2. That's amazing! He's broken the world record!

4. "Go! Go! Go!" roared the crowd as the quarterback sped toward the end zone.

EXERCISE 22.1 Using apostrophes to signal possession

2. *Lindsay's* boyfriend, Evan, is a sous chef at one of *Boston's* trendiest restaurants.

4. *Evan's* ears perked, however, when I told him I'd been reading cookbooks and watching cooking shows.

6. Although I want to have my own cookbook collection one day, my local *library's* cooking section is impressive.

8. The fancy kitchen store near my apartment carries all sorts of amateur and advanced home *cooks'* tools.

10. Even though I'm a novice at the stove, I agree with Evan that most *dishes'* success lies in the power of their ingredients.

EXERCISE 22.2 Using apostrophes appropriately

2. Please ask where we're going so we don't get lost.

4. That guy who's been giving you a ride after work called at about nine o'clock.

6. The bike I'm riding to school isn't new, but it's in good shape.

8. The distributor says that your order has not received its approval from the business office.

10. That cat of yours is nothing but trouble.

EXERCISE 23.1   Using quotation marks to signal direct quotation

2. C

4. Yesterday, the president told Congress, "Democrats and Republicans need to cooperate."

6. C

8. "Ours is the most imaginative generation in recent history," he wrote.

10. "Is the computer plugged in?" the technical support operator asked, prompting Harry to snarl, "Yes, I'm not a complete idiot."

EXERCISE 23.2   Using quotation marks for titles and definitions

2. My dictionary defines *isolation* as "the quality or state of being alone."

4. Kowinski uses the term *mallaise* to mean "physical and psychological disturbances caused by mall contact."

6. "The little that is known about gorillas certainly makes you want to know more," writes Alan Moorehead in his essay "A Most Forgiving Ape."

8. If you had ever had "Stairway to Heaven" running through your head for four days straight, you would not like Led Zeppelin either.

10. Amy Lowell challenges social conformity in her poem "Patterns."

EXERCISE 23.3   Using quotation marks appropriately

SUGGESTED ANSWERS

2. Television commercials have frequently used popular songs as an effective way to connect their product with good feelings in consumers' minds.

4. The strategy of using hit songs in commercials can backfire when the listeners don't like the song or like it too much to think of it as an advertising jingle.

6. The rights to many Beatles songs, such as "Revolution," are no longer controlled by the Beatles.

8. Many Iggy Pop fans wonder what on earth his song "Lust for Life" has to do with taking an expensive ocean cruise.

10. Do consumers love the songs of their youth so much that merely hearing a song in an ad will make them buy that car?

EXERCISE 24.1   Using parentheses and brackets

2. Generally, most acknowledge that first-born children (including only children) show a greater sense of responsibility and self-confidence.

4. However, experts have not yet proven (through reliable scientific studies, that is) that these generalizations are true.

6. Initial studies indicate that middle children may have an increased risk of developing certain health problems (including depression and chronic fatigue syndrome [CFS]).

8. However, this conclusion (like most claims relating to birth order) has been questioned.

10. Clearly, more research is needed if we want to resolve the "contradictory findings and long-standing conceptual disagreements" that characterize the debate about birth order and intelligence (Sulloway 1711).

EXERCISE 24.2   Using dashes

2. Nevertheless, extra charges seem to be added to more and more services all the time.

4. The hidden costs of service fees are irritating—people feel that their bank accounts are being nibbled to death.

6. The "convenience charges" that people have to pay when buying show tickets by telephone are often a substantial percentage of the cost of the ticket.

8. C

10. C

EXERCISE 24.3   Using colons

2. C

4. The sonnet's structure is effective in revealing the speaker's message: love has changed his life and ended his depression.

6. The filmmakers clearly knew what the audience wanted: adventure, suspense, and romance.

8. C

10. Every week, my father watches his favorite television shows: *The Office*, *Lost*, and *Dancing with the Stars*.

EXERCISE 24.5   Reviewing punctuation marks

2. Nowadays, even high school students are fearlessly diving in and attempting to make a profit from their unique ideas.

4. Such classes often provide fundamentals—such as writing, speaking, and accounting—but they also give students the opportunity to develop and implement their own business plans.

6. Many instructors who teach these classes receive training from the National Foundation for Teaching Entrepreneurship (NFTE).

8. Mr. Mariotti says that entrepreneurship classes empower students and teach them academic skills at the same time.

10. As an increasing number of high schools are adding entrepreneurship studies to the curriculum, many colleges and universities are doing the same.

12. At a few particularly business-oriented colleges, all students are required to practice, in one way or another, being entrepreneurs.

14. Babson gives each class of twenty-five to thirty students money to put its plans into action; all profits go to charity.

16. Students from these universities will often go on to start nonprofit organizations that work to eliminate poverty or to improve education.

18. They call entrepreneurship programs "trendy," and claim that these classes simply train students to be "good capitalists."

20. C

EXERCISE 25.1 Capitalizing

2. The Battle of Lexington and Concord was fought in April 1775.

4. Accepting an award for his score for the film *The High and the Mighty*, Dmitri Tiomkin thanked Beethoven, Brahms, Wagner, and Strauss.

6. We drove east over the Hudson River on the Tappan Zee Bridge.

8. "Bloody Sunday" was a massacre of Catholic protesters in Derry, Northern Ireland, on January 30, 1972.

10. The town in the American South where I was raised had a statue of a Civil War soldier in the center of Main Street.

EXERCISE 26.1 Using abbreviations

2. The power tools, ordinarily used for sanding wood, are placed on a thirty-foot track and plugged in; the sander to reach the end first wins.

4. There are three divisions of belt sander races: the stock division, which races sanders right out of the box; the modified division, which allows any motor the owner wants to add; and the decorative division, which provides a creative outlet for sander owners.

6. The fastest sanders run on very coarse sandpaper—a number sixteen grit is an excellent choice if it's available.

8. The S-B Power Tool Co. in Chicago, maker of Bosch sanders, allows participants to race its tools, but the company does not underwrite races.

10. No one knows what percentage of the nation's power tools have been used for this kind of entertainment.

EXERCISE 26.2 Spelling out numbers and using figures

SUGGESTED ANSWERS

2. You could buy any item in the store for ninety-nine cents. (*Or* C)

4. C

6. Because gas was $4.39 a gallon, she decided not to go.

8. Three hundred seven miles long and eighty-two miles wide, the island offered little of interest.

10. The department received 1,633 calls and 43 letters.

EXERCISE 27.1 Using italics

2. Regional writers produced some American classics, such as Mark Twain's *Huckleberry Finn* and James Fenimore Cooper's *Last of the Mohicans*.

4. Some of the most prolific regional writers were women such as Kate Chopin, who wrote her first collection of short stories, *Bayou Folk*, to help support her family.

6. Chopin also departed from regional works to explore women's experiences of marriage, as in her short piece, "The Story of an Hour."

8. She later turned these into a novel, *Deephaven*, which she hoped would "teach the world that country people were not . . . ignorant."

10. Many regional stories—Stephen Crane's "The Bride Comes to Yellow Sky" is a prime example— show the writer's concern that an isolated culture is in danger of disappearing.

EXERCISE 28.1   Using hyphens in compounds and with prefixes

2. thirty-three

4. the all-American soccer team

6. C

8. self-guided

10. cutting-edge technology

EXERCISE 28.2   Using hyphens appropriately

2. The name of the president-elect had been announced an hour before the polls closed.

4. C

6. The ill-fated antelope became the baboon's lunch.

8. The badly wrapped sandwich oozed mustard and bits of soggy lettuce.

10. C

LANGUAGE

EXERCISE 30.1   Identifying stereotypes

2. *how few hours*: Overlooks all the other work academics do in addition to classroom teaching: grading, conferencing, committee work, research.

4. *everyone in France hates Americans*: Overlooks the fact that like people everywhere, people in France are individuals with widely varying points of view about Americans (and every other topic).

6. *Dropouts*: Assumes anyone who didn't finish high school chose not to finish and is therefore foolish, unmotivated, lazy, or (perhaps) a criminal.

8. *Goths and trench coats*: Assumes that all young people who wear trench coats are Goth or have certain dark, morbid views. Also, assumes all Goths and trench coat wearers are dangerous (carrying guns, knives, bombs, etc.).

EXERCISE 30.3   Rewriting to eliminate offensive references

SUGGESTED ANSWERS

2. My friend is going to teach me sign language.

4. State representative Greg Smith won the election yesterday.

6. Violinist Josh Mickle, last night's featured soloist, brought the crowd to its feet. (Age and religion are both irrelevant here.)

8. Please tell my assistant that I would like to meet at three o'clock today.

10. You can call a plumber to fix the sink.

EXERCISE 32.1 Using formal register

SUGGESTED ANSWERS

2. He decided to buy his ticket while the prices remained reasonable.

4. We decided not to buy a bigger car that got poor gas mileage and chose instead to keep our old Honda.

6. After she had raced to the post office at ten minutes to five, she realized that she had completely forgotten the fact that it was a federal holiday.

8. Moby Dick's enormous size was matched only by Ahab's obsessive desire to destroy him.

10. The class behaved so dreadfully in their regular teacher's absence that the substitute lost his temper.

EXERCISE 32.2 Determining levels of language

SUGGESTED ANSWERS

2. formal; *audience*: readers motivated to learn about student loans

4. formal; *audience*: an informed audience that you hope to convince

EXERCISE 32.3 Checking for correct denotation

2. carnivore, not carnival

4. attached, not detached

6. prey, not pray

8. C

10. agreement, not argument

EXERCISE 32.4 Revising sentences to change connotation

2. waltz away/little people who keep the company running/peanuts
   Rewrite: CEOs are highly compensated with salary, stock options, and pensions while employees get comparatively little.

4. Tree-huggers/ranted
   Rewrite: Environmentalists protested the Explorer's gas mileage outside the Ford dealership.

6. riddled/peddling/hogwash
   Rewrite: Many Internet sites offer unreliable information.

8. mob/yelling/jabbing
   Rewrite: A large group of chanting, sign-waving protesters appeared.

EXERCISE 32.5 Considering connotation

SUGGESTED ANSWERS

2. *girl*: young lady, miss

4. *abide*: tolerate; *turns*: changes; *vital*: alive; *hold still*: contain their energy

EXERCISE 32.6 Using specific and concrete words

SUGGESTED ANSWERS

2. The Frick Museum in New York City features well-known paintings by great European and American artists, such as El Greco, Edgar Degas, and James McNeill Whistler. The Frick collection also includes sculptures, eighteenth-century French furniture, and Oriental rugs.

4. The Smollings' children rarely get invited to other peoples' homes because they squabble constantly, demand endless adult attention, break dishes, and jump on furniture.

6. Robert had a fever of 103 degrees and a rasping cough, so he stayed home from the holiday party at his office.

8. The feast at Mom's on Sunday was delicious as usual: roast chicken, garlic and sage stuffing, sweet garden peas, gallons of gravy, and half a fresh-baked apple pie each.

10. Few places in the United States display the wild climatic variations of central Texas: at one moment, the sky may be clear blue and the air balmy; at another, a racing flash flood may drown the landscape and threaten lives.

EXERCISE 32.7 Thinking about similes and metaphors

SUGGESTED ANSWERS

2. *great mounds of marshmallow fluff* (metaphor): clarifies the white and fluffy appearance of the clouds

4. *as if someone had punched him in the stomach* (simile): compares an emotion with a physical feeling

6. *like a magnolia corsage* (simile): makes vivid and concrete Mom Willie's heritage and suggests how positively she values it—and how proudly she "displays" it

8. *like water moving in a cavern* (simile): compares the sound of the waitress's voice to water in a cavern, helping the reader to imagine the sound

10. *lounging* (metaphor): compares the horse in pasture to people relaxing; *cuddling up* (metaphor): emphasizes the pleasure the writer has reading mysteries; *top priority* (metaphor): reading as an activity of official importance

MULTILINGUAL WRITERS

EXERCISE 34.1 Expressing subjects and objects explicitly

SUGGESTED ANSWERS

2. C

4. There are problems with doing everything online, of course.

6. There are small-time thieves and pranksters disrupting online services.

8. A hacker can get enormous amounts of online data, even if the site is supposed to be secure.

10. Internet users must use caution and common sense online, but it is also essential for online information to be safeguarded by security experts.

EXERCISE 34.2 Editing for English word order

SUGGESTED ANSWERS

2. He displays a flag proudly in the window.

   Or

   He proudly displays a flag in the window.

4. She should not go into the woods alone.

6. The train arrives promptly at six o'clock.

8. I like to go to the movies with friends.

10. "Spend your money carefully," advised my mother.

EXERCISE 35.2 Using appropriate noun phrases

2. Dangerous germs, such as salmonella, are commonly found in some foods.

4. Many people regularly clean their kitchen counters and cutting boards to remove bacteria.

6. Every time someone wipes a counter with a dirty sponge, more germs are spread around the kitchen.

8. According to research studies, young single men's kitchens tend to have fewer germs than other kitchens.

EXERCISE 36.1 Identifying verbs and verb phrases

2. Holi is known as the festival of colors, not only because spring brings flowers, but also because Holi celebrations always include brightly colored dyes.

4. During Holi, people toss fistfuls of powdered dyes or dye-filled water balloons at each other and sing traditional Holi songs.

6. Any person who is walking outside during a Holi celebration will soon be wearing colored powders or colored water.

8. Many people wear white clothing for Holi.

10. Doesn't Holi sound like fun?

EXERCISE 36.3   Using specified forms of verbs

POSSIBLE ANSWERS

2. Someone followed the instructions too literally.
   Someone was following us as we drove to the beach.

4. The geese migrated to avoid a harsh winter.
   The geese are migrating late this year.

6. Those teenagers consumed three dozen hamburgers and two cases of pop.
   When I left the picnic, the teenagers were consuming the last of the carrot cake.

8. My father cooks dinner every night.
   Our father was cooking pancakes when we got up this morning.

10. Some artists work at night while others prefer to work in the morning.
    Local artists had worked together on the mural, and the community loved the result.

EXERCISE 36.4   Identifying tenses and forms of verbs

2. had beaten: past perfect

4. have asked: present perfect

6. danced: simple past

8. has driven: present perfect

10. had forgotten: past perfect

EXERCISE 36.5   Using verbs appropriately

2. The Rosetta Stone is *covered* with inscriptions in three ancient languages.

4. At that time, scholars *had been* puzzled by hieroglyphics for centuries.

6. A scholar named Jean François Champollion could *understand* both ancient Greek and modern Egyptian, known as Coptic.

8. From the Demotic inscription, he *learned* to read the hieroglyphics.

10. The hieroglyphics and the Demotic and Greek texts all *contain* a decree from an ancient king.

EXERCISE 36.6   Using infinitives and gerunds appropriately

SUGGESTED ANSWERS

2. Ashok refused to answer his sister's questions.

4. C

6. We appreciated getting the invitation.

EXERCISE 36.7   Writing conditional sentences

Suggested answers

2. If the dot-com boom had continued, that prediction might have come true.

4. If any computer job is announced these days, hundreds of qualified people apply for it.

6. If Indian workers required as much money as Americans do to live, U.S. companies would not be as eager to outsource computer work to the other side of the world.

8. Would fewer Americans be unemployed right now if the dot-com boom had never happened?

10. If American students want to prepare for a secure future, they should consider a specialty such as nursing, in which jobs are available and the work cannot be sent abroad.

EXERCISE 37.1   Using prepositions idiomatically

2. in

4. in

6. on

8. with

10. to

EXERCISE 37.2   Recognizing and using two-word verbs

2. two-word verb

4. two-word verb

6. verb + preposition

8. two-word verb

10. two-word verb